THE WORLD IN NUMBERS

Over 2,000 Figures and Facts

Written by
Steve Martin, Clive Gifford
and Marianne Taylor

Illustrated by Andrew Pinder

Edited by Jen Wainwright
With thanks to Philippa Wingate
Design by Barbara Ward
Cover design by John Bigwood

Revised paperback edition first published in 2017
First published in Great Britain in 2013 by Buster Books,
an imprint of Michael O'Mara Books Limited, 9 Lion Yard,
Tremadoc Road, London SW4 7NQ

 www.busterbooks.co.uk Buster Children's Books @BusterBooks

A CIP catalogue record for this book is available from the British Library.

ISBN: 978-1-78055-478-5

2 4 6 8 10 9 7 5 3 1

Papers used by Buster Books are natural, recyclable products made from
wood grown in sustainable forests. The manufacturing processes
conform to the environmental regulations of the country of origin.

This book was printed in May 2017 by Leo Paper Products Ltd,
Heshan Astros Printing Limited,
Xuantan Temple Industrial Zone,
Gulao Town, Heshan City,
Guangdong Province, China

THE WORLD IN NUMBERS

Over 2,000 Figures and Facts

Buster Books

Contents

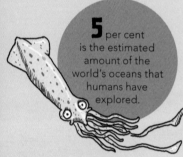

80 aircraft were shot down by World War I's most successful fighter pilot – a man called Manfred von Richthofen.

5 per cent is the estimated amount of the world's oceans that humans have explored.

4

12

110.4 kilograms of pure gold was used to make a coffin for an Egyptian pharaoh called Tutankhamun.

84

500 years is the lifespan of a mythical bird known as a phoenix.

58 was the size of the enormous clown shoes worn by Coco the Clown.

42

50 kilograms was how much a knight's armour could weigh.

150

Introduction

Are you ready to get knocked out by numbers and flabbergasted by facts and figures?

1 metre is the length a walrus's tusks can grow to.

21

1 outfit was the only set of clothes King Frederick II of Prussia owned in his later years, besides his military uniforms.

This book will take you on a roller-coaster ride – through history, around the world, into the animal kingdom, to outer space and beyond!

90 seconds or less is all it takes the Terrafugia Transition® flying car to fold up its wings after landing and drive away like a regular motor vehicle.

42

536 minutes is the amount of time that astronauts Susan Helms and Jim Voss spent outside their spacecraft on a spacewalk in 2001.

4

59 kilograms is all that the smallest car on sale weighs.

Each page is packed with fascinating facts to boggle your brain. You'll amaze your friends with your new-found knowledge. Whether you dip in and out, picking out the tastiest morsels, or read every page from beginning to end, you're sure to find dozens of facts that will make you say, **'Wow!'**

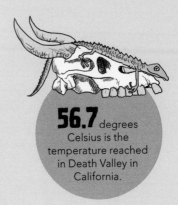

56.7 degrees Celsius is the temperature reached in Death Valley in California.

13

What are you waiting for? Dive in and discover the world in numbers.

900 grams is the weight of the biggest recorded African giant snail.

Terrific Treasure

20 metres is the length, width and height of a cube that you could make from putting together all the gold that has been discovered in the world.

46 million dollars was the price paid by a jeweller called Laurence Graff for a beautiful pink diamond now known as The Graff Pink.

100,000 people joined a famous 19th-century rush to the Klondike River area of Canada, when gold was discovered there.

1 diamond mine in the USA will let you become a diamond miner for a day. The Crater of Diamonds State Park in the USA will allow you to mine there and keep any diamonds you can find.

100 million dollars' worth of diamonds and precious gems were stolen in Belgium during a famous robbery from the Antwerp Diamond Centre in 2003. The treasure has never been found.

3,245 years is how long the treasure from the tomb of Tutankhamun, an Egyptian pharaoh, lay undisturbed before it was found by an archaeologist called Howard Carter in 1922.

105 diamonds were made from the largest diamond ever discovered – The Cullinan, found in South Africa in 1905. These diamonds are now part of the British Crown Jewels.

4,350 men set off on a South American expedition in 1540 to find some legendary treasure. It was said that the people of a lost city, led by their chieftan, called El Dorado, had thrown treasure into a lake, as an offering to the gods. The city has never been found.

7,590,020 dollars were once paid for a single gold coin – a 1933 Double Eagle from the USA – in a 2002 auction.

80 per cent of the world's gold still lies underground, waiting to be found.

60 countries in the world have gold mines.

24-carat gold was used to make a full-size golden toilet at the Hang Fung Gold Technology Group showroom in Hong Kong.

8 out of an original **50** jewelled eggs, made by a craftsman named Peter Carl Fabergé, are now missing. Made for the Russian royal family, each Fabergé egg is exquisitely decorated, so the missing eggs are worth tens of millions of dollars.

181 pieces of jewellery decorated the world's most expensive Christmas tree.

6.4 kilograms was the weight of the largest pearl ever found.

600,000 silver coins were salvaged from the wreck of the codenamed *Black Swan*, a 17th-century shipwreck that was found off the coast of Spain in 2007.

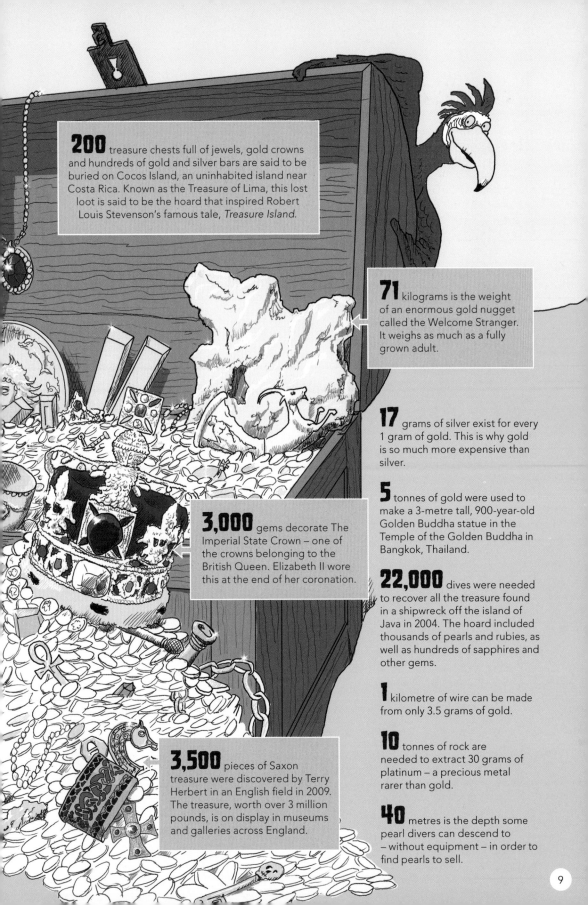

200 treasure chests full of jewels, gold crowns and hundreds of gold and silver bars are said to be buried on Cocos Island, an uninhabited island near Costa Rica. Known as the Treasure of Lima, this lost loot is said to be the hoard that inspired Robert Louis Stevenson's famous tale, *Treasure Island*.

71 kilograms is the weight of an enormous gold nugget called the Welcome Stranger. It weighs as much as a fully grown adult.

17 grams of silver exist for every 1 gram of gold. This is why gold is so much more expensive than silver.

5 tonnes of gold were used to make a 3-metre tall, 900-year-old Golden Buddha statue in the Temple of the Golden Buddha in Bangkok, Thailand.

3,000 gems decorate The Imperial State Crown – one of the crowns belonging to the British Queen. Elizabeth II wore this at the end of her coronation.

22,000 dives were needed to recover all the treasure found in a shipwreck off the island of Java in 2004. The hoard included thousands of pearls and rubies, as well as hundreds of sapphires and other gems.

1 kilometre of wire can be made from only 3.5 grams of gold.

10 tonnes of rock are needed to extract 30 grams of platinum – a precious metal rarer than gold.

3,500 pieces of Saxon treasure were discovered by Terry Herbert in an English field in 2009. The treasure, worth over 3 million pounds, is on display in museums and galleries across England.

40 metres is the depth some pearl divers can descend to – without equipment – in order to find pearls to sell.

Disgusting Dinners

900 different flavours are available at an ice cream shop in Venezuela. The strangest is spaghetti and cheese ice cream.

40 metres is the height the durian tree can grow to. It bears a fruit that has such a horrible stink that it is banned from many public places in southeast Asia.

70,000 crushed cochineal bugs are used to make 450 grams of red dye. This dye is then used to colour food, including sweets.

50 dollars is what you might have to pay for 1 cup of the world's priciest coffee. Kopi Luwak coffee is made from beans which have been eaten and then pooed out by small, cat-like animals called civets.

37.8 degrees Celsius is the temperature needed to melt a waxy substance found in sheep's wool known as lanolin. One of its uses is as an ingredient in chewing gum.

36 cockroaches were eaten by Ken Edwards in 1 minute.

2 of the worst jobs in history were carried out by slaves at Roman feasts. The spittle collector mopped up all the spit, and the vomit collector had to collect all the vomit after the Romans were sick from too much eating.

26,470 dollars was the fine given to a food company when a man found a dead mouse inside his loaf of bread.

14 helpings of dessert, plus lobster, kippers, caviar and sauerkraut (pickled cabbage) caused the death of the King of Sweden in 1771.

11.3 metres was the length of a tapeworm found in Sally Mae Wallace. Diners can accidentally swallow tapeworms if they eat undercooked meat. The parasites can then grow and grow inside a person's intestines. Yuck!

100-year eggs, also called century eggs, are a Chinese delicacy. The eggs are preserved in salt, lime and ash (although not for as long as 100 years) until the yolk turns green and smells of sulphur.

7 of the most disgusting jelly bean flavours you can buy are bogey, dirt, vomit, earwax, earthworm, rotten egg and soap.

8 millimetres is the length that live maggots in Casu Marzu cheese can grow to. The maggots crawl around inside the cheese, and if they're disturbed they can jump, too. The maggot-infested cheese is so disgusting it is illegal … but that doesn't stop people eating this traditional Sardinian food.

7.5 centimetres is the length to which Madagascar hissing cockroaches can grow. Injected with honey and soy sauce, these crispy critters are served as a snack by a chef in the USA.

500 auk birds are placed inside a seal skin and left for several months to make the Greenland dish Kiviak. A favourite way to eat the food is to bite the bird's head off and suck out its insides.

107.1 decibels was the rating of the world's loudest belch by Paul Hunn in 2008. That's louder than a farm tractor.

15 strong-smelling cheeses were put through a stink test by scientists to find the world's smelliest cheese. The winner was a French cheese known as Vieux Boulogne.

1 litre of blood is used to make enough black pudding for 4 people. The food is a traditional, much-loved British breakfast ingredient – the blood is mixed with fat, onions, oatmeal, herbs and butter.

25-centimetre-long wooden skewers are used to hold the meat for the American treat of 'Alligator on a Stick'.

3 sizes of crab – small, medium or large – are available from live crab vending machines in China.

2 animals were needed to make the medieval dish of roast cockatrice. This is because a cockatrice was an invented creature made by sewing half a pig to half a rooster.

2 cups of duck's blood is the main ingredient in duck blood soup, a popular dish in Poland.

4–6 weeks is how long salmon heads are buried in the ground before being dug up and eaten. This Alaskan dish of rotten fish is often known as 'stink heads'.

14 farts per day is the average per person. For extra … er … aroma, eat plenty of beans, cabbage, cheese, and eggs!

191 degrees Celsius is the temperature of the oil that chocolate is fried in for the Scottish dish of deep-fried chocolate bar. To make sure the chocolate doesn't melt it is coated in batter.

2 popular flavours – raspberry and vanilla – are sometimes manufactured from a substance called castoreum, which comes from a beaver's bum. It is used to flavour sweets, ice-cream, jelly and yoghurt.

30 insect fragments per 100 grams of peanut butter is the average allowed by American Food and Drug Administration laws. Crunchy!

60 per cent protein is contained in the nutritious Mexican dish of escamoles. The meal also tastes very nice … as long as you don't mind eating ants' eggs.

The Moon

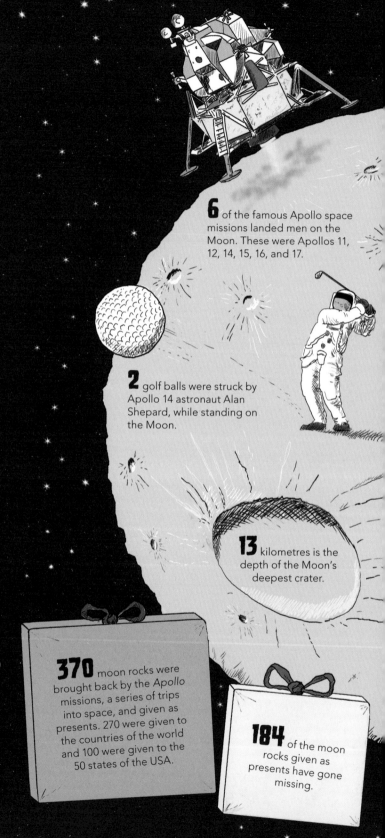

27.3 days is how long it takes the Moon to rotate on its axis and to orbit the Earth. This is why we always see the same face of the Moon.

107 degrees Celsius is the maximum temperature of the Moon on its sunny side. That's hot enough to boil water.

384,400 kilometres is the average distance of the Moon from the Earth.

3.8 centimetres is how much further away the Moon gets from the Earth each year.

9 years is how long it would take to walk to the Moon at an average walking speed of 4.8 kilometres per hour.

4.5 billion years is the age of the Moon.

442,500 dollars were paid for just 0.2 grams of Moon dust in 1993.

1.3 seconds is how long it takes for light to travel from the Moon to the Earth.

2 high tides occur every day on every coastal beach on Earth because of the Moon's pull on the oceans.

20 seconds worth of landing fuel was all that remained when Apollo 11 finally touched down on the Moon after a 4-day journey from the Earth.

6 of the famous Apollo space missions landed men on the Moon. These were Apollos 11, 12, 14, 15, 16, and 17.

2 golf balls were struck by Apollo 14 astronaut Alan Shepard, while standing on the Moon.

13 kilometres is the depth of the Moon's deepest crater.

370 moon rocks were brought back by the *Apollo* missions, a series of trips into space, and given as presents. 270 were given to the countries of the world and 100 were given to the 50 states of the USA.

184 of the moon rocks given as presents have gone missing.

1 small step for man, **1** giant leap for mankind. These were the words spoken by an astronaut called Neil Armstrong when he became the first man to walk on the Moon.

3 Lunar Roving Vehicles have carried astronauts across the Moon's surface.

4,700 metres is the height of Mons Huygens, the tallest mountain on the Moon (just over half as high as Mount Everest).

13 per cent of people who took part in a 1988 survey actually thought the Moon was made of cheese!

3,474 kilometres is the diameter of the Moon. The Earth's diameter is 12,742 kilometres, making it over 3.5 times bigger.

8 phases of the Moon complete its cycle. These are: new Moon, waxing crescent, first quarter, waxing gibbous, full Moon, waning gibbous, third quarter and waning crescent. The cycle then begins all over again.

6 kilograms of weight on Earth would only weigh 1 kilogram on the Moon.

2,500 kilometres is the width of the widest craters on the Moon.

29.5 days is how long it takes to get from one full moon to the next. This is called the lunar cycle.

72.5 million kilometres around the Sun is the distance the Earth travels while the Moon makes 1 orbit of the Earth.

-233 degrees Celsius is the temperature at the coldest points on the Moon, at the bottom of craters which are always in shadow and never get any sunlight.

4 other moons in the Solar System are bigger than our Moon.

50 Moons could fit inside the Earth if it was hollow.

Mother and Baby

1 female is all you need to start a colony of whiptail lizards, because they can reproduce without needing any males.

5 years of devoted parental care is given to a baby orangutan by its mum.

30 tiny baby Tasmanian devils can be born in a single litter, but the mother only has 4 teats, so most of the babies will starve and only the strongest survive.

3 months is how long baby polar bears may spend in a den, dug into the snow by their mother. They come out for the first time in early spring.

50 per cent of a whale's milk is made up of fat.

31.7 to **34.5** degrees Celsius is the temperature range at which crocodile eggs need to stay for the babies to be males. If the eggs are any cooler or warmer, they will be female.

29 eggs, laid by a grey partridge, made up the largest clutch of birds' eggs ever recorded.

1,500 baby seahorses may be born in one go. It is the male that gives birth to them.

3.5 years is the length of time a frilled shark's pregnancy lasts.

35,000 eggs may be produced by a female cane toad each time she spawns.

85 per cent of the time, a mother free-tailed bat finds her own baby among the 3,000 that are hanging around in the breeding cave. The rest of the time, she ends up with another bat's baby.

4 babies, genetically identical quadruplets, are born in each litter of nine-banded armadillos.

85 grams is the weight of a newborn giant panda, just 0.13 per cent of its mother's weight.

6 centimetres is the length of an adult paradoxical frog. But, as a tadpole, it is much bigger at 16.8 centimetres long.

8 metres is the length of a newborn blue whale. It weighs 2,700 kilograms. It will grow to 30 metres long and can weigh as much as 81,000 kilograms.

1 egg is all that a female Cuban frog produces, but she takes great care of it.

25 baby scorpions can fit on their mum's back. She carries them around all the time to keep them safe from danger.

DELICIOUS!

2 baby black eagles hatch out in each nest, but the older one almost always kills the younger one.

1 year is how long a mother earwig spends taking care of her offspring. That's around half her lifetime.

161 female fur seals in a colony may all have pups fathered by the same male.

1 species of mammal is known to have males that produce milk. It's the Dayak fruit bat of Malaysia.

14 litters a year can be produced by a female house mouse, with 7 babies in an average litter.

1.8 metres is the height of a newborn giraffe.

4 is the average number of babies produced by an alpine salamander, after her 38-month pregnancy. She starts off with up to 60 babies growing inside her, but the oldest ones eat the rest during the pregnancy.

20,000 baby emperor penguins can live in a breeding colony. When the mother penguins return from fishing, they each have to find their own baby among all the others.

3 months is how long a bromeliad crab guards and feeds her babies – no other species of crab provides any care at all to their offspring.

5 weeks is the age at which a young quail (a type of small bird) can start having babies of its own.

Fabulous Feasts

65 hard-boiled eggs were eaten in 6 minutes and 40 seconds by a competitive eater called Sonya Thomas.

20,000 people hurl 120,000 kilograms of tomatoes at each other during the annual food fight in Buñol in Spain.

3,600 kilograms of krill (a small, shrimp-like creature) is a blue whale's daily diet.

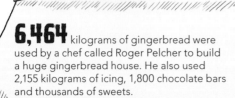

6,464 kilograms of gingerbread were used by a chef called Roger Pelcher to build a huge gingerbread house. He also used 2,155 kilograms of icing, 1,800 chocolate bars and thousands of sweets.

12 dishes representing the signs of the zodiac were part of a feast described in a book called the Satirycon by an ancient Roman writer, alongside dormice, a hare with wings and a whole calf wearing a helmet.

269 elephants ate 50 tonnes of fruit and vegetables during an elephant parade held in Thailand in 2003.

42 peanut butter and jelly sandwiches were eaten in just 10 minutes by Patrick Bertoletti in 2007.

6,014 seats are available in Syria's Damascus Gate Restaurant, so there's no need to reserve a table.

50,000 kilograms of fish can be eaten during the Helsinki Herring Fair, held in Finland to celebrate the end of the fishing season.

45 million turkeys are eaten in 1 day in the USA during Thanksgiving.

22,295 officials feasted at The Banquet of Mayors, held in Paris in 1900. 3,600 chefs were needed to prepare all the food.

24 hours was all it took for the ancient Romans to transport fresh oysters from north-west France to Rome via a network of chilled carts. Fresh oysters were prized as a delicacy.

7,395 metres above ground was the height of the dinner party held in a hot-air balloon by 3 men in England in 2005. They dressed in formal dinner clothes and dined on poached salmon at temperatures as low as −50 degrees Celsius.

4 animals are used for the main dish at wedding feasts of the Bedouin people. The dish is a roast camel stuffed with a whole roast sheep, stuffed with a chicken, stuffed with fish, stuffed with eggs. Phew!

30 minutes was all it took Britain's Queen Victoria to eat her way through 7 courses at her banquets. All the plates were cleared each time she finished a course, so the guests had to try to keep up with her.

1 glass of wine allowed Cleopatra, an Egyptian queen, to win a bet with the Romans to see who could hold the most expensive banquet. She simply dissolved her expensive pearl earring in a glass of wine, and then drank it.

60.3 metres was the length of a single hot dog made by the Shizuoka Meat Producers of Japan. That is as long as 34 adult men lying head-to-toe.

600 ostriches were used to make ostrich pies for a huge feast given by the Roman Emperor Elagabalus.

10 tonnes was the weight of a single curry cooked by the Eastern Eye restaurant in England.

2,000 sheep were eaten at a feast to celebrate a meeting between the English and French kings. It was held at a place known as the Field of the Cloth of Gold in 1520, and the feasting lasted for a whole month.

9,852 slices of toast were used to make a giant toast mosaic of a woman's face. The picture was made by toasting the bread so that it created different shades, ranging from white, to light brown, to dark brown, to black.

4 kilometres was the length of the tables at a street party in China in 2008. 3,050 tables were placed end-to-end for the diners to sit at.

9,137 litres of coffee filled a huge coffee mug in Las Vegas. That's enough for over 32,000 normal-sized cups of coffee.

32,681 people sat down and drank a cup of tea together at a huge tea party held in India.

7,500 varieties of apple are grown throughout the world.

7 kilograms of garlic was what it cost to buy a healthy male slave in ancient Egypt – this shows that garlic was really valuable!

37.4 metres was the diameter of a pizza made in South Africa in 1990. That's about 4 times longer than a London bus.

Europe

10 European countries have monarchs. The European royal families are in Belgium, Denmark, Liechtenstein, Luxembourg, Monaco, the Netherlands, Norway, Spain, Sweden and the UK.

7 countries are home to the Alps mountain range. These are Switzerland, Austria, Italy, Liechtenstein, Germany, France and Slovenia.

1,500 different types of sausage can be eaten in Germany.

227 islands are home to the population of Greece, as well as the Greek mainland itself.

5,642 metres is the height of Russia's Mount Elbrus. It is the highest mountain in Europe.

26 per cent of Holland lies below sea level and 60 per cent of the population live in this area. The sea is kept at bay by 2,400 kilometre-long embankments called dykes.

1 million underwater wooden supports called piles are thought to support a church called the Santa Maria della Salute in Venice, Italy. The piles are needed for buildings as the city was built over the sea.

HELP!

2.25 billion seeds can be stored at the Global Seed Vault on the remote Norwegian island of Svalbard. The seeds are stored at −18 degrees Celsius and can last hundreds or even thousands of years. This means that the world has seeds in safe storage should there ever be a global catastrophe.

6 European countries have German as an official language: Germany, Switzerland, Austria, Luxembourg, Belgium and Liechtenstein.

50 countries make up the continent of Europe.

53 per cent of Europeans speak more than one language.

35 volcanoes are active on the small island of Iceland.

3 European countries insist cars are driven on the left-hand side of the road – the United Kingdom, Ireland and Cyprus.

400 ships pass through the Dover Strait – a narrow stretch of sea between England and France – every single day.

8,400 square kilometres is the size of Vatnajokull, Europe's largest glacier. It is in Iceland, and has an average ice thickness of 900 metres.

56 per cent of the water used by the people of Malta, a Mediterranean island, has to be produced from sea water (using a process called desalination). The country has no rivers at all.

225 European languages are spoken.

90 per cent of Europe was once covered by forests. Today, the figure is only 33 per cent.

100 per cent of Iceland's heating and electricity comes from renewable sources. Most comes from hydro (water) power, but some is generated from the heat inside the Earth and is called geothermal power.

17 million square kilometres is the size of Russia, Europe's largest country.

0.44 square kilometres is the size of the Vatican State in Rome.

This means Europe has both the largest and the smallest countries in the world.

9 countries share a border with Germany. These are: Denmark, the Czech Republic, Austria, Poland, Switzerland, France, Luxembourg, Belgium and the Netherlands.

0 deserts are in Europe, making it the only continent in the world not to have one.

3,530 kilometres is the length of Russia's River Volga, from source to sea. It's the longest river in Europe.

4 European countries lie partly in the Arctic Circle. These are Russia, Norway, Sweden and Finland.

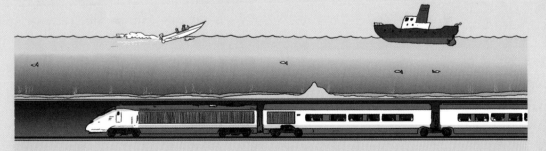

50 kilometres is the length of a railway tunnel, called the Channel Tunnel, which connects England with France. 38 kilometres of the tunnel is under the sea.

The Titanic

269.1 metres was the length of the Titanic – longer than 2.5 full-sized football pitches.

3,423 sacks of letters and parcels were carried onboard the Titanic. They were looked after by the ship's own post office, staffed by 5 workers.

94 per cent of the women and children who were travelling in first class survived the sinking of the Titanic.

22.5 knots (41.6 kilometres per hour) was the cruising speed of the Titanic just before it struck an iceberg in the Atlantic Ocean.

1 indoor heated swimming pool was found on board, one of the first of its kind.

15 pounds, **10** shillings was the cost of the transatlantic trip for a servant of a first-class passenger. That's more than £600 in today's money.

473 third-class passengers could eat in the sparse, simple dining room. They were served bread, fresh fruit and simple meals such as roast beef and boiled potatoes.

73 years after sinking, the wreck of the Titanic was discovered on the floor of the Atlantic Ocean.

11 courses, including oysters, roast duckling and chocolate eclairs, were served to first class passengers on the night that the Titanic hit an iceberg.

0 passenger lifeboat drills were carried out during the Titanic's voyage.

64,000 pounds was the price that a lunch menu from the Titanic was sold for at auction.

15 tonnes was the weight of the Titanic's largest anchor – around the same weight as 10 motor cars.

3 of the ship's **4** giant funnels actually worked. 1 of them was fake and was added to make the ship look more impressive.

10,000 lightbulbs lit up the ship's many rooms, decks and corridors.

157 minutes after it struck the iceberg, the Titanic's hull broke into 2 parts.

20 lifeboats were carried on the ship but they only provided enough space for half of the passengers and crew on board.

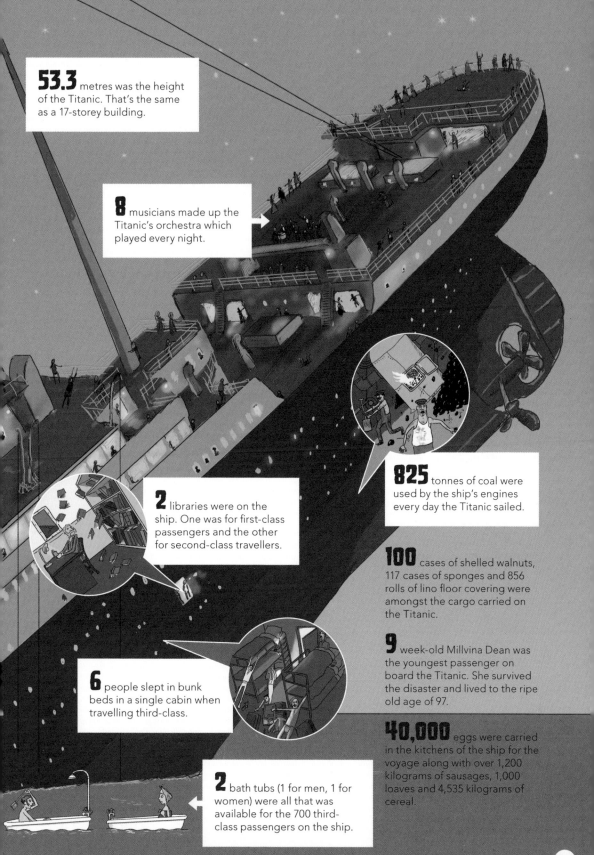

53.3 metres was the height of the Titanic. That's the same as a 17-storey building.

8 musicians made up the Titanic's orchestra which played every night.

825 tonnes of coal were used by the ship's engines every day the Titanic sailed.

2 libraries were on the ship. One was for first-class passengers and the other for second-class travellers.

100 cases of shelled walnuts, 117 cases of sponges and 856 rolls of lino floor covering were amongst the cargo carried on the Titanic.

9 week-old Millvina Dean was the youngest passenger on board the Titanic. She survived the disaster and lived to the ripe old age of 97.

6 people slept in bunk beds in a single cabin when travelling third-class.

40,000 eggs were carried in the kitchens of the ship for the voyage along with over 1,200 kilograms of sausages, 1,000 loaves and 4,535 kilograms of cereal.

2 bath tubs (1 for men, 1 for women) were all that was available for the 700 third-class passengers on the ship.

Super Snakes

1 in every **500** people living in the Ryuku islands in the Pacific is bitten by a snake every year.

20 minutes is your life expectancy if a black mamba gets its fangs into you, unless you find medical help.

5-centimetre-long fangs make the gaboon viper truly fearsome.

100 metres is the distance that the paradise tree snake can glide through the air, making it look like it's flying.

110 milligrams of venom from an inland taipan is enough to finish off 100 people, or 250,000 mice.

30 minutes is how long a Burmese python can stay underwater without coming up for air.

120 of the **180** species of snake in Australia are venomous.

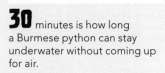

1,134 kilograms is the estimated weight of the biggest ancient snake species, the gigantic 13-metre-long *Titanoboa*.

5.6 metres is the record length for a king cobra – the longest venomous snake.

10.8 centimetres is the length of an adult thread snake, the smallest kind of snake.

600 species of snake are venomous.

2,500 species of snake are harmless.

5 hours or more are needed for a python to swallow its prey.

7.67 metres was the length reached by one enormous reticulated python.

1/3 of a king cobra's body can be lifted off the ground to attack its large prey.

12 hours is how long it can take for you to feel the effects of a bite from the very venomous coral snake.

80 eggs may be laid by a female python in one batch.

60 centimetres is the size of a baby green anaconda just after it's born. It will grow to up to 9 metres in length.

60 times per second is the speed a rattlesnake can shake the rattle on the end of its tail.

4 weeks after a big dinner, a boa constrictor starts to think about its next meal.

5 years is the record amount of time a type of Asian viper can go without food.

100 per cent of snakes are meat eaters.

30 per cent of snake species give birth to live babies.

70 per cent of snake species lay eggs.

450 small bones make up the spine of a snake.

100 kilometres was the length of a line of sea snakes that was spotted in 1932. Millions of the snakes were swimming together.

I THINK SOMEBODY'S FOLLOWING ME ...

Making Music

88 keys make up a standard piano keyboard. There are 52 white and 36 black keys.

4 metres is the length a French horn would be if it was uncoiled.

3 metres in height and over 227 kilograms in weight explain why the University of Texas's bass drum is called Big Bertha. It is wheeled around and played at marches and football matches.

6 is the usual number of strings on a guitar, but they can also have 4, 7, 8, 9, 10 or 12.

1,000 years is the length of time a piece of music called *Longplayer* will last for. The piece has been playing since 31st December 1999.

33,112 pipes make the Atlantic City Convention Hall organ a huge and incredibly loud musical instrument.

4 families of instruments are in an orchestra. These are the strings, brass, woodwind and percussion instruments.

90,000 guitar strings are made every single day by the Fender guitar company.

54.96 metres was the combined length of the five metal pipes that were used to make a huge wind chime in Illinois, USA.

2 is the number of times in Scottish history that the bagpipes have been banned. In fact, poor James Reid was actually executed in 1746 for playing the bagpipes!

46 centimetres of goatskin are stretched over a frame to make the Irish drum known as the Bhodran.

11 musicians are in The Vegetable Orchestra, a musical group that plays a range of instruments all made out of vegetables.

450 kilograms is the amount a Steinway Grand Piano can weigh.

4 million dollars was the value of a high quality violin called a Stradivarius that was left in a taxi in 2008. The violinist was so pleased when the driver returned it that he gave him a free concert.

6 millimetres is the tiny size of the smallest maker of a musical instrument – a termite which hollows out the wood used to make the traditional Australian instrument known as the didgeridoo.

1 million harmonicas are made every year by Hohner, the world's biggest manufacturer of the instrument.

1,120 minutes is the length of time it takes to play *Vexations* by Erik Satie. When it was first played in New York, only one audience member managed to sit through the entire performance.

1 string is all that the Indian instrument, the ektara, uses. The player plucks it while changing the tension of the string to alter its sound.

2,134 ukulele players once performed together in a huge musical jam in Yokohama, Japan.

230 strings are found in a typical piano.

182 centimetres is the length of each bar of a huge xylophone know as the doso. Normal xylophone bars are usually no longer than a few centimetres.

152 centimetres is the length of the longest string on a typical harp, which can have up to 47 strings.

0 instruments are needed to play the composer John Cage's piece called *4'33"* because it consists of 4 minutes and 33 seconds of complete silence.

30 violins are included in a typical symphony orchestra.

5 lines are used to write music down, this is called a stave. This method of noting down musical notes first appeared in Italy in the 13th century.

3 valves on a trumpet allow the musician to play 45 different notes.

7 different positions for a trombone slide produce a range of different notes.

260 calories are burned for every hour that you play the drums. That's twice as many as when playing the guitar.

70 pieces of wood are used to make a violin.

4 main instruments make up the string section of an orchestra: the violin, viola, cello and double bass.

The Deep Blue Sea

99 per cent of the planet's living space is taken up by the oceans.

71 per cent of planet Earth is covered by water.

50 quadrillion tonnes is the estimated amount of salt in the sea. If the salt was removed and spread out over the Earth's surface it would form a layer that was taller than a 40-storey building.

10,898 metres is the depth of a valley called Challenger Deep in the Mariana Trench – the lowest point on Earth.

97 per cent of the Earth's water is made up by the oceans.

600,000 barrels of oil, on average, are accidentally spilled into the sea from ships every year.

35 grams of salt are contained in 1 litre of sea water.

3.5 billion people rely on the sea for the food they eat.

75 per cent of the world's largest cities can be found at the seaside.

20 billion kilograms of gold is found in tiny particles in the world's sea water. It would be very, very expensive to try and extract it all though.

35 degrees Celsius is the temperature of the hottest part of the ocean, in the Persian Gulf.

–1.8 degrees Celsius is the freezing point of most sea water.

10,000 metres is the height of Mauna Kea. It is the tallest mountain in the world, if you ignore the fact that 5,996 metres of it is under the sea.

5 per cent is the estimated amount of the world's oceans that humans have explored. That means there are countless deep sea species that are yet to be discovered.

121 metres is the depth of the deepest dive achieved by a person without any breathing equipment.

400 different species of coral are found on the Great Barrier Reef in Australia.

16.3 metres is the difference between high and low tide at the Bay of Fundy in North America, the home of the world's highest tides.

46,000 pieces of plastic are found floating in every 2.5 square kilometres of the world's oceans.

524 metres was the height above sea level that waters reached after a tsunami – that's 5 times the height of the Statue of Liberty. This massive wave of water struck Lituya Bay, Alaska in 1958.

84 chemical elements are present in sea water.

330 metres is the deepest dive ever made by a scuba diver.

80 per cent of the pollution in the ocean comes from people's activities on land.

400 degrees Celsius is the temperature that may be reached by water that is pumped out of hydrothermal vents. These are openings in the sea floor. Because these vents are usually about 2 kilometres deep, pressure from the weight of sea above stops the water from boiling.

33 per cent of the Dead Sea is salt. In most sea water it is more like 3.5 per cent. This makes the sea water in the Dead Sea very dense, so swimming in it feels more like floating.

3,795 is the average depth of the sea in metres.

165.25 million square kilometres is the size of the Pacific Ocean. That's bigger than all the land on Earth put together.

66 is the number of metres that the sea level would rise if all the ice in the world melted.

3.54 kilometres is the height of the world's biggest under-sea waterfall. It is 3.5 times taller (and much, much slower) than the tallest waterfall on land.

8 tonnes per 6.5 square centimetres is the water pressure at the deepest point in the ocean. That's the same as 1 person trying to lift 50 jumbo jets!

25,000 islands can be found in the Pacific Ocean.

90 per cent of the Earth's volcanic activity happens under the sea.

2,300 kilometres is the length of the Great Barrier Reef in Australia.

Myths and Legends

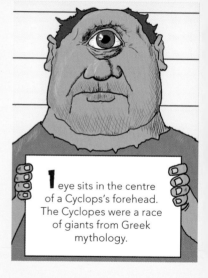

5 of the planets in our Solar System were discovered by the Romans. These are Mercury, Venus, Mars, Jupiter and Saturn. They named them after gods they worshipped. Neptune is also named after a Roman god, but this planet wasn't discovered until 1846.

120 paces was the distance from which a man named William Tell shot an arrow at his son. He had to hit an apple that was on his son's head.

8 legs belonged to a horse called Sleipnir, which was ridden by a Norse god called Odin.

1 eye sits in the centre of a Cyclops's forehead. The Cyclopes were a race of giants from Greek mythology.

3 types of giant existed in Norse mythology – mountain giants, frost giants and fire giants.

7 voyages are described in the adventures of Sinbad the Sailor.

7 young men and **7** young women were sacrificed each year to a mythical monster with the head of a bull called the Minotaur. This continued until a Greek hero called Theseus entered the monster's labyrinth (maze) and killed the creature.

2 leather purses are carried by creatures called leprechauns in Celtic mythology. 1 purse holds a silver coin that returns to the purse every time it is spent and the other holds a gold coin used to bribe anyone who captures the leprechaun – the coin later turns to ash.

25 knights' names are written on the Winchester Round Table. This is thought to be the round table from a famous British legend about King Arthur and his Knights of the Round Table.

40 thieves were outwitted by a merchant's son called Ali Baba. He learned a magic password, Open Sesame, that allowed him to break into a cave and steal the thieves' treasure.

8 dangerous levels of the underworld had to be crossed by the dead in Aztec mythology before they found peace in the ninth layer.

4 dwarves held up the 4 corners of the sky in Norse mythology – Austri (east), Vestri (west), Nordri (north), and Sudri (south).

52-year cycles caused terror to the Aztecs who believed that the world could end at the end of each cycle. They carried out rituals such as destroying their possessions to try to stop it from happening.

60 hours a week are spent on the waters of a lake in Scotland called Loch Ness by a man called George Edwards. He has spent his life searching for a monster who is believed to live in the lake.

540 doors allowed Viking heroes slain in battle to enter the heavenly hall of Valhalla, ruled over by the god Odin.

3 brothers ruled the world in Roman mythology. Jupiter ruled the sky, Neptune ruled the sea and Pluto ruled the underworld.

500 years is the lifespan of a mythical bird known as a phoenix. At the end of its long life, it sets fire to its nest and dies, so that a brand new phoenix can arise from the ashes.

3 wise monkeys are mentioned in Japanese folklore. They are called See No Evil, Hear No Evil and Speak No Evil.

38,000 strange, hexagonal stone columns can be seen at the Giant's Causeway in Northern Ireland. Legend tells that a giant, Finn McCool, built a path across the sea to Scotland so he could fight his rival, the giant Benandonnar.

1 coin was placed with a dead body by mourners in ancient Greece. They believed the corpse could use this to pay a ferryman to take him across the River Styx to the underworld.

12 labours (tasks) had to be carried out by Hercules, a hero in Greek and Roman legend. These included slaying monsters and capturing beasts and treasures from across the globe.

5 claws belonged to the Celestial Dragon, the ruler of all Chinese dragons, according to myth in China. Only the Emperor was permitted to wear a symbol of a 5-clawed dragon. Anyone else foolish enough to do so was put to death.

2 faces belonged to Janus, a Roman god of entrances, who could see both forwards and backwards. The month of January is named after him as it is the entrance to a new year.

10 years was the length of a legendary siege called the Trojan War, between the Greeks and the Trojans. The Greeks won when they hid warriors inside a giant wooden horse, which was left outside the city gates as a present for the Trojans.

4 legs at dawn, **2** legs at noon, **3** legs in the evening. What is it? This riddle was asked by the ancient Greek Sphinx to passing travellers who were killed if they answered incorrectly. (The answer is a human being, who crawls as a baby, walks as an adult and uses a walking stick in old age.)

1,001 Nights is a collection of oriental legends. A king called Shahryar married and killed a new wife each day until one new queen began telling stories. The king enjoyed them so much he decided not to kill her.

Wild Cats

MMM ... DELICIOUS!

5.4 metres is the highest recorded jump for a puma.

30 lions belong to the Savuti pride in Botswana. There are enough of them to regularly team up and kill elephants.

250 pounds was what it cost to buy a lion cub from a famous London shop called Harrods in the 1960s.

5 is the number of species of 'true' big cats or 'roaring cats' – the lion, tiger, leopard, snow leopard and jaguar.

6 baby antelopes were adopted by a confused Kenyan lioness called Kamunyak. She stole them from their mums and tried to take care of them herself.

85 different kinds of animals may be eaten by a hungry hunting jaguar.

2.5 years is the average time a male lion will be in charge of a group, called a pride, before another male kicks him out.

YOU HOLD IT AND I'LL COUNT THEM.

600 is about the average number of spots on a cheetah.

384 kilograms was the weight of the heaviest tiger ever recorded. That's about 85 times heavier than a normal house cat.

8 is the largest litter of cubs a cheetah mum can have.

20 centimetres was the length of a prehistoric, sabre-toothed cat's huge, canine teeth.

650 people are mauled or killed by wild big cats each year.

8 kilometres is the distance over which a lion's roar can be heard.

96 kilometres an hour is the top recorded speed for a cheetah running flat-out.

436 people died at the claws and teeth of a wild cat known as the Champawat Tigress in India, before she was shot dead in 1907.

20 minutes is the time it takes a cheetah to get its breath back after a 20-second chase at full speed.

114 decibels is how loud a lion's roar can be. That's louder than the speakers at a rock concert.

3,500 years ago, Egyptian people started to keep wild cats as pets, giving rise to the moggy that's so popular today.

1.5 kilograms is the average weight of a rusty-spotted cat, the smallest wild cat in the world. The average pet cat weighs about 4.5 kilograms.

1,500 people were killed over 15 years in the 1930s and 1940s by a pride of man-eating lions in Tanzania.

0 tigers have identical stripes. Each tiger's coat is unique – like a human's fingerprint.

25 kilograms of meat may be consumed by a jaguar at 1 meal. That's like you eating 100 quarter-pounder burgers at 1 sitting.

5,000 tigers live in captivity in North America, compared to just 3,200 in the wild in the whole of Asia.

293 square kilometres is the size of Iriomote Island. It's the only place where a rare species called the Iriomote cat lives.

200 Siberian tigers are left in the wild.

15 metres is the distance (longways) that a snow leopard can jump – that's 7 times its own body length.

120 kilograms of prey can be carried in the jaws of a 60-kilogram leopard as it climbs up a tree.

41 species of wild cat exist in the world today.

0 rare snow leopards were seen by an author called Peter Matthiessen, when he travelled to their native lands in Asia to research his book *The Snow Leopard*.

Puma   Cougar   Mountain lion   Indian devil

40 different names are used for the puma, including cougar, mountain lion and Indian devil.

The Wild West

5 dollars was all it cost to buy a plot of land in the centre of a legendary Wild West town called Tombstone when it was founded in 1879.

1,048 grams is the weight of a Colt Peacemaker revolver – a gun commonly used by Wild West sheriffs and the outlaws they tried to stop.

0 buffalos were shot by Buffalo Bill (real name William Cody) in his lifetime. The animals Cody did shoot were American bison.

28 stagecoach robberies were credited to an outlaw known as Black Bart (real name Charles Bolton). He often wore a mask made from an old flour sack with eye holes cut out of it.

66 years after being shot and killed, an outlaw called Elmer McCurdy was finally buried. His body had been preserved and had been used as a prop in plays and even early TV shows.

66 camels were imported from Egypt by the US Army in 1856 to use as pack animals. They were later sold to a circus.

0.252 seconds is the fastest timed quick draw of a gun from its holster, performed by Howard Darby in Canada in 2000. Quick draw shooting (with blanks instead of bullets) is a popular competition in some parts of North America.

2 aces, along with the **8** of clubs and **8** of spades were some of the cards that Wild Bill Hickock was holding in his hand during a game of poker, when he was shot dead in a saloon. These cards have been known since as the dead man's hand.

30 seconds was the length of a gunfight at the OK Corral between the Clanton gang and the Earp brothers and their ally, Doc Holliday. The shootout left 3 gunfighters dead.

720,000 Winchester Model 1873 rifles were manufactured. This gun was commonly used by cowboys and earned the nickname, the gun that won the West.

30 paces away from her target, Annie Oakley was such a good shot that she could hit the thin edge of a playing card with a bullet every time.

41 million dollars' worth of gold (worth around 1 billion dollars today) was mined in California's Wild West in 1850.

1 million mustangs (wild horses) and over 5 million cattle were herded along a track called the Chisholm Trail by cowboys between 1867 and 1884.

23 bullets hit an outlaw called Emmett Dalton in a shootout with lawmen in 1892, but he survived. After serving 14 years in prison for his crimes, he became an actor and estate agent.

10,000 dollars was the reward for the capture of 2 outlaws called Frank and Jesse James offered on an 1881 poster by the Governor of Missouri. The reward was never collected.

1 member of the US 7th Cavalry Regiment survived a bloody clash called the Battle of the Little Bighorn in 1876. The survivor was a horse called Comanche.

35,000 letters and other mail were carried by Pony Express horse riders in 1860–61. They rode between Missouri and California, a distance of over 2,800 kilometres, and only ever lost 1 mail bag.

3,500 workers produced 2 million Stetson hats a year in the early 1900s. The Stetson was first designed by John Batterson Stetson in 1865 and became the cowboy hat of choice soon after.

16 was the number of years sharpshooting Annie Oakley toured with Buffalo Bill's Wild West show, entertaining thousands of people with her accurate trick shooting.

6 was the usual number of bullets that could fit into a revolver – often worn in a leather holster, or tucked into a cowboy's belt.

10 years old was the age of a famous Native American chief called Sitting Bull when he killed his first bison.

2 days' water supply, plus food for many weeks, was carried by a chuck wagon, a mobile kitchen for cowboys. Cowboys were often served up simple meals involving beef, pork, beans, potatoes and cornbread.

30-60 million bison roamed the plains of the United States at the start of the 19th century. Large-scale hunting for their hides and their meat reduced their population to mere hundreds by 1900.

Australia and Oceania

14 countries are included in the continent of Australia and Oceania. These are: Australia, New Zealand, Papua New Guinea, Fiji, Micronesia, the Marshall Islands, Samoa, the Solomon Islands, Tonga, Kiribati, Nauru, Tuvalu, Vanuatu and Palau.

2,228 metres is the height of Australia's highest mountain, Mount Kosciuszko in New South Wales.

7 times more sheep live in New Zealand than humans.

14 per cent of New Zealanders are Maoris – the original native inhabitants of the country.

5,531 kilometres is the length of a single fence, known as the Dingo Fence, which runs from South Australia to Queensland.

750,000 wild camels roam the outback, giving Australia more wild camels than any country in the world.

9 islands make up the country of Tuvalu. The total size of these tiny, remote islands is only 27 square kilometres.

600 islands make up the Great Barrier Reef, a huge coral reef in Australia. It is the only living thing on Earth visible from space.

332 islands make up the country of Fiji. 110 of these are inhabited.

4 metres is the height that Australian termite mounds can reach. These amazing structures are built by insects that are only about 5 millimetres long.

836 different languages are spoken in Papua New Guinea.

3,720 kilometres long, Australia's Murray-Darling River is the longest river on the continent.

3.6 kilometres long, **2.4** kilometres wide and **348** metres high, Uluru is one of Australia's best-known landmarks. It is also known as Ayers Rock.

146 kilometres is how long a road in Australia's Nullarbor Plains stretches without a single turn. This makes it the longest section of straight road in the world.

100 different aboriginal languages are still spoken in Australia.

34,000 square kilometres is the size of Anna Creek Station, an enormous cattle ranch in South Australia. That's bigger than the country of Belgium.

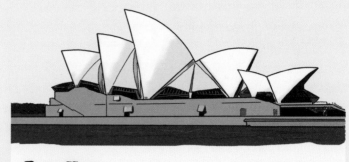

8 million people visit the famous Sydney Opera House every year.

25 million kangaroos live in Australia.

48 kilometres per hour is the speed at which emus can run. These large birds are only found in the wild in Australia.

120-kilometre-long Fraser Island, off the Australian coast, is the largest sand island in the world.

35,877 kilometres is the length of mainland Australia's coastline.

21 square kilometres make Nauru the continent's smallest country.

140 different species of marsupial live in Australia and most of them cannot be found anywhere else. Marsupials are mammals whose young are carried in a pouch on the mother's belly. Examples of marsupials include kangaroos, wombats and koalas.

1,600 kilometres is the distance from New Zealand to its nearest neighbour, Australia.

2,104 kilometres is the distance you would have to travel from Perth, in Western Australia, to reach the nearest major city with a population of over 1 million, Adelaide. That's about the same distance as travelling from London, England, to St Petersburg, Russia.

4 out of **5** Australians live near the coast.

427.2 metres was how far a boomerang was thrown at Murarrie Recreation Ground, Queensland, Australia in 2005. That's further than the length of 4 soccer pitches.

Plants and Trees

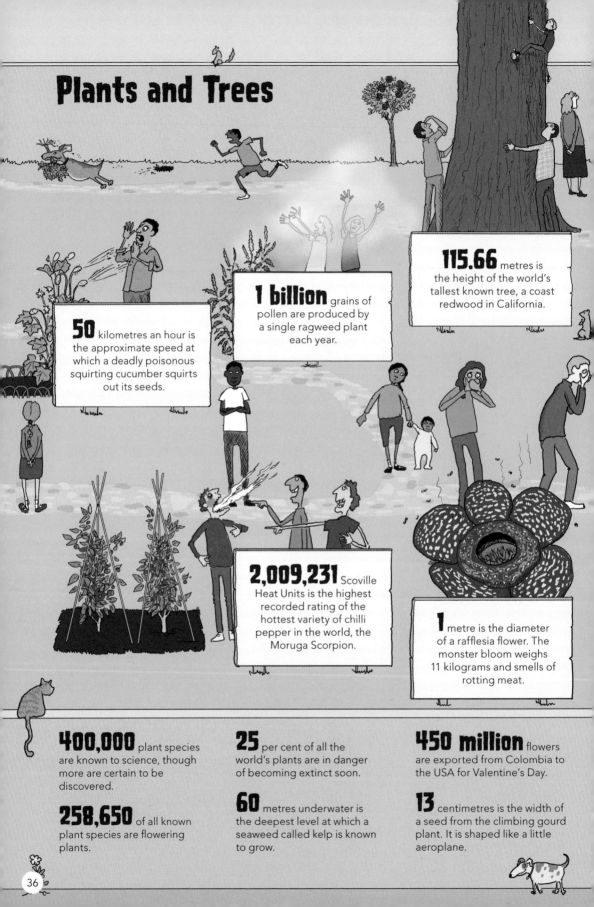

50 kilometres an hour is the approximate speed at which a deadly poisonous squirting cucumber squirts out its seeds.

1 billion grains of pollen are produced by a single ragweed plant each year.

115.66 metres is the height of the world's tallest known tree, a coast redwood in California.

2,009,231 Scoville Heat Units is the highest recorded rating of the hottest variety of chilli pepper in the world, the Moruga Scorpion.

1 metre is the diameter of a rafflesia flower. The monster bloom weighs 11 kilograms and smells of rotting meat.

400,000 plant species are known to science, though more are certain to be discovered.

258,650 of all known plant species are flowering plants.

25 per cent of all the world's plants are in danger of becoming extinct soon.

60 metres underwater is the deepest level at which a seaweed called kelp is known to grow.

450 million flowers are exported from Colombia to the USA for Valentine's Day.

13 centimetres is the width of a seed from the climbing gourd plant. It is shaped like a little aeroplane.

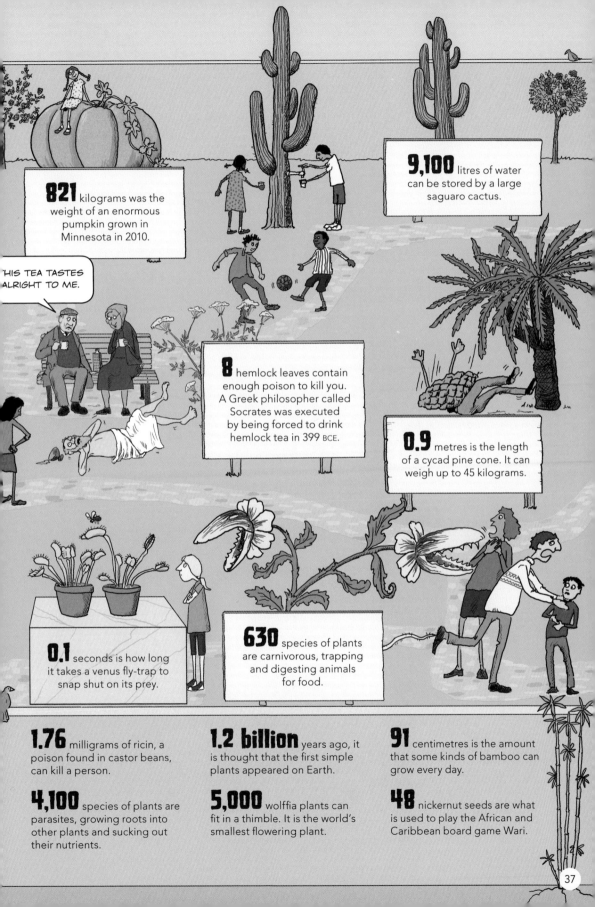

821 kilograms was the weight of an enormous pumpkin grown in Minnesota in 2010.

9,100 litres of water can be stored by a large saguaro cactus.

THIS TEA TASTES ALRIGHT TO ME.

8 hemlock leaves contain enough poison to kill you. A Greek philosopher called Socrates was executed by being forced to drink hemlock tea in 399 BCE.

0.9 metres is the length of a cycad pine cone. It can weigh up to 45 kilograms.

0.1 seconds is how long it takes a venus fly-trap to snap shut on its prey.

630 species of plants are carnivorous, trapping and digesting animals for food.

1.76 milligrams of ricin, a poison found in castor beans, can kill a person.

4,100 species of plants are parasites, growing roots into other plants and sucking out their nutrients.

1.2 billion years ago, it is thought that the first simple plants appeared on Earth.

5,000 wolffia plants can fit in a thimble. It is the world's smallest flowering plant.

91 centimetres is the amount that some kinds of bamboo can grow every day.

48 nickernut seeds are what is used to play the African and Caribbean board game Wari.

Marvellous Monarchs

209 kilograms was the weight of Tonga's King Taufa'ahau Tupou IV in 1976. He was judged to be the world's heaviest monarch.

19 brothers and half-brothers of Mehmed III, a ruler of the Ottoman Empire, were executed in 1595 on his orders.

50 per cent of the population of the island of Madagascar are thought to have been killed during the reign of murderous Queen Ranavalona.

413 beds could be found in the palaces of the French King Louis XIV.

108 children who survived infancy were born to Fat'h Ali Shah Qajar, the Emperor of Persia. There were 60 boys and 48 girls.

78,000 Christmas puddings have been given by British Queen Elizabeth II to her staff.

1.1 million people have attended garden parties held by British Queen Elizabeth II at Buckingham Palace or Holyrood House.

5 million square kilometres is believed to be the size of the empire of an ancient Greek ruler called Alexander the Great.

> AIM! FIRE!

10 centimetres was the length of a tiny silver cannon Queen Christina of Sweden had built to combat her fear of fleas!

> THERE'S DEFINITELY ONE ELEPHANT MISSING ...

1 set of clothes was the only outfit King Frederick II of Prussia owned in his later years, besides his military uniforms.

20 minutes was the reign of King Louis XIX of France. He abdicated (quit) as king after less than half an hour.

30,204 days is the longest known reign of a monarch. This record is held by King Sobhuza II of Swaziland.

12,000 elephants were owned by Emperor Jahangir of India in the 17th century.

4,936 diamonds were found in a crown worn by Empress Catherine of Russia at her coronation in 1762.

28 emperors of China have died between the ages of 10 and 19.

THIS COUNTS AS ONE MEAL, RIGHT?

2 was the maximum number of meals a day people were allowed to eat in England after Edward III passed a law in 1336.

376 horses and **117** footmen accompanied Marie-Antoinette on her journey to France, where she would marry the heir to the French throne.

10 billion US dollars were donated by Abdullah bin Abdulaziz Al Saud, ruler of Saudi Arabia, to a university in 2008.

5,300 breeding pairs of mute swans live in the UK, and they all officially belong to Queen Elizabeth II.

16 petals on a golden Chrysanthemum make up the badge of the Japanese Emperor.

700,000 workers built an underground city that would house the Chinese Emperor Qin Shi Huang when he died. He was buried with thousands of life-sized warriors made of clay.

3 years into his reign as King of Hungary, Béla I died when the wooden throne he sat on collapsed.

COULD WE HAVE SOMETHING ELSE FOR TEA TOMORROW?

450 kilograms was the weight of an enormous wheel of cheese given to British monarch, Queen Victoria, as a wedding present. That's about as heavy as an adult horse.

132 centimetres is thought to have been the size of King Henry VIII's waist just before his death. That's almost twice the size of a wine barrel at its widest point.

4 different Emperors ruled the Roman Empire in a single year, CE 69.

110.4 kilograms of pure gold was used to make a coffin for an Egyptian pharaoh called Tutankhamun.

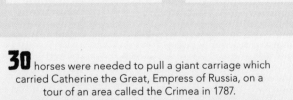

30 horses were needed to pull a giant carriage which carried Catherine the Great, Empress of Russia, on a tour of an area called the Crimea in 1787.

Terrific Technology

204.1 million emails were sent every minute in 2011.

8–10 was the maximum number of 3- to 4-minute-long MP3 songs you could store on the world's first portable MP3 player, the MPMan F10. It went on sale in 1998, 3 years before the first iPod.

0.025 millimetres (less than the width of a human hair) is the length of the world's smallest playable guitar, the Nanoguitar II. It has to be played with a microscopic laser though, not your fingers.

NOBODY MOVE! I THINK I DROPPED IT ...

240 kilometres per hour is the top speed reached by the Formula Rossa roller coaster at Ferrari World in Abu Dhabi.

3,500 degrees Celsius (35 times the boiling point of water) is the temperature that the Odeillo solar furnace, in France, can reach. The furnace uses giant mirrors to focus sunlight on to a small area to heat it up to really high temperatures.

9 years of an average American's life will be spent watching television.

13 tonnes – which is almost the weight of 3 adult elephants – was the weight of the Univac 1, the first commercially available computer.

5,127 different prototypes (early versions) of a vacuum cleaner were built and tested by James Dyson before he finally perfected his famous bagless design.

30 minutes was the battery life of the very first mobile cellular phone developed by Motorola in 1973. It took 10 hours to recharge the battery of the chunky phone, which weighed 1.1 kilograms.

130 was the total number of websites on the World Wide Web in June 1993. Today, there are over 1 billion.

14.83 US dollars was the price paid for the very first item sold on an auction website called eBay. It was a broken laser pointer. Today, a mobile phone is sold every 21 seconds on the site.

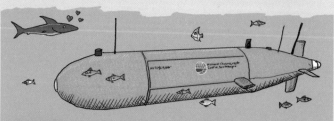

5,000 torch batteries are used to power an underwater robot called the Autosub 3. It can dive up to 1,600 metres below sea level and travel underwater for up to 60 hours in 1 voyage.

51.9 million
computers were disposed of in the United States in 2010.

2.9 days was the time it would have taken to download a 9MB music file in the 1980s. People used a device called an acoustic coupler, which connected early computers to a telephone line.

14 days, **22** minutes and **8** seconds was how long a flying robot called the Qinetiq Zephyr managed to continue flying without landing in 2010.

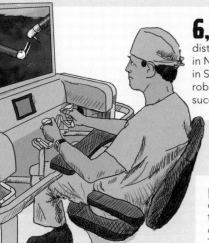

6,200 kilometres was the distance between surgeons in New York and their patient in Strasbourg, France, when a robot was used to perform a successful operation in 2001.

2,520 giant solar panels, each the size of a house, work together at the Moura Photovoltaic solar power station in Portugal. They take in energy from the Sun and generate enough electricity to supply 30,000 homes.

59 kilograms is all that the smallest car on sale, called the Peel P50, weighs. The vehicle is 1.37 metres long, seats 1 person and has no reverse gear. To park it, you get out and pull it into place by hand.

1 millimetre was the size of a complete computer built by researchers at the University of Michigan, USA. The minuscule device has memory, a battery and a tiny processor – the brain of the computer.

60,000 years is the amount of time it would take 1,000 people, each performing a maths calculation every second, to complete the same number of calculations that a Cray Titan supercomputer can perform in a single second.

6 games of chess were played between Deep Blue, a chess-playing computer, and Gary Kasparov, the human chess champion. It was a close match, but the computer won in the end.

Brilliant Bees

20,000 different species of bees live on planet Earth.

4 years is the average lifespan for a queen honey bee, but her workers live just a few weeks.

4 days after a queen bee lays an egg, the egg hatches.

3 minutes after a bee stings you, the stinger finally finishes pumping its venom into the wound. So scrape the sting out quickly!

170 different smells can be detected by honey bees.

1,100 bee stings at the same time will probably kill you.

90,000 kilometres is the distance travelled by a bee to gather 500 grams of honey.

8 is the shape that honey bees make when they dance, to show the other bees where to find nectar.

2 tablespoons of honey would give a bee enough energy to fly around the world.

4 centimetres is the length of a Wallace's giant bee. It's the biggest in the world.

2 millimetres is the length of the Trigona duckei bee from Brazil – the world's smallest species.

19 body segments make up a bee's body – 6 form the head, 3 the thorax (between the neck and the rest of the body) and 10 the abdomen (the bee's body).

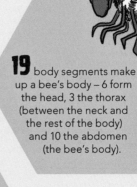

1 in **3** of the mouthfuls of food we eat only exists because of bees and other insects pollinating crops.

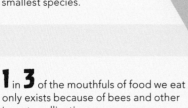

5 eyes are on a bee's head – 2 big ones and 3 tiny ones.

11,000 wingflaps every minute cause the buzzing sound you can hear when bees fly.

54 kilometres per hour is the flight speed of a bumblebee in a hurry.

24 kilometres per hour is the fastest a honey bee can fly.

1 or **2** per cent of people are allergic to bee stings.

304 calories are in every 100 grams of honey.

14 degrees Celsius is the temperature at which honey starts to crystallize.

10 segments make up a female bee's antenna, but a male has 11.

6 degrees Celsius is the lowest air temperature that a bumblebee can fly in, but it will first have to shiver for 15 minutes to warm itself up enough for the flight.

400 kilometres a year is the speed at which the African bees known as killer bees have spread across South and Central America.

60,000 bees live in the average bee colony.

225 bees a day are caught and eaten by a bird called the bee-eater.

80–85 per cent of honey is pure sugar.

0.1 milligrams of venom are injected into you when a honey bee stings you.

48 hours is how long it takes a honey bee to get back to normal after drinking alcohol. They drink nectar from fermented fruit and sometimes steal sips of beer or wine from people's glasses. Drunk bees cannot walk or fly straight, and they poke their tongues out.

60 centimetres is the depth to which a mining bee may dig its burrow.

500g

0.08 teaspoons of honey are gathered by the average worker bee in its lifetime.

2 million flowers have to be visited by bees to gather the pollen for just 500 grams of honey.

Wicked Weather

1,800 thunderstorms are probably happening somewhere in the world while you read this.

119 kilometres per hour is the speed at which wind officially becomes a hurricane.

15 tonnes is the amount of water in a typical, small, fluffy cloud.

1.2 metres of rain typically falls on the town of Mawsynram in India each year. It's the rainiest place on Earth.

200 fog-filled days every year make Grand Banks in Newfoundland, Canada, the foggiest place in the world.

120 million tonnes of soil were blown on to Chicago, USA, during a blizzard in 1934.

2 rainbows can sometimes form in the same place at the same time. When this happens, the second rainbow will be fainter, but its colours will appear in reverse order.

2 weeks' worth of power for a typical house is contained in a single lightning bolt.

30,000 degrees Celsius is the temperature that can be reached inside a bolt of lightning.

218,000 kilometres per hour is the speed a bolt of lightning can travel.

353 kilometres was the distance travelled across the USA by a tornado in 1935.

1.825 metres is the height of a tall man, and yet this is the depth of rain that fell in a single 24-hour period on the island of La Réunion in the Indian Ocean.

1,200 tornadoes strike the USA every year, more than any other country on Earth.

21,000 metres is the height of the biggest thunderclouds, known as cumulonimbus clouds.

1 hour is how long it can take a snowflake to fall to the ground.

1 kilogram was the weight of a hailstone that came crashing to Earth in Bangladesh in 1986.

56.7 degrees Celsius was the blisteringly hot temperature reached in 1913 in the suitably-named Death Valley in California.

1,400 trillion litres of water are evaporated each day on our planet.

400 years is how long some places in Chile's Atacama Desert have waited without seeing any rain.

187 days of continual daylight (when the Sun is constantly above the horizon) occur at the North Pole – followed by 178 days of continual darkness.

4,267 metres was the height that a pilot called Curtis Talbot flew to in order to create the first man-made snowstorm in 1946. He released dry ice into the clouds, and the snowflakes started to fall.

31 metres of snow fell in just 1 year in Mount Rainier in the USA.

34.6 metres was the height of Angus, a giant snowman, built in Maine, USA. This means he was about the height of a 10-storey building. He was so large he had trees for arms.

-89.2 degrees Celsius is the coldest temperature ever measured on Earth. It was recorded at Vostok in Antartica, whose warmest ever temperature was a freezing –19 degrees.

Ancient Egypt

4 sacred jars were used during the embalming process of a dead body to store the liver, lungs, stomach and intestines after they had been removed.

11 pharaohs (rulers) of ancient Egypt were given the name Ramesses, meaning Born of the sun-god Ra.

2 eyebrows were often shaved off to show grief by an ancient Egyptian when their pet cat died.

6 Cleopatras were queen of Egypt before the most famous Cleopatra, the one who became the last pharaoh of Egypt, came to power in around 51 BCE.

10 days made up a week in ancient Egypt. Many workers only got 1 day off every week or 2 weeks … and you think school is bad!

20 metres is the height of each of the 4 giant statues of the pharaoh Ramesses II found outside a temple dedicated to him at Abu Simbel – that's 3 times taller than an adult giraffe!

102 lions were claimed to have been killed by the pharaoh Amenhotep III using arrows.

140 metres of material were used to wrap a mummy.

139 walking sticks made of ebony wood, ivory, silver and gold were found in the tomb of Tutankhamun. That's not all! Buried in King Tut's tomb were also 6 chariots, 2 thrones and all sorts of other items.

700 different remedies and potions for illnesses are described on the Ebers Papyrus – an amazing ancient Egyptian medical text. These included mixing a pig's eye with other ingredients to help make a blind person see again.

52.4 was the approximate length in centimetres of the cubit. This was a measurement used widely in ancient Egypt, which was based on the length of an adult's arm from the elbow to the fingertips.

1,224 pieces of an ancient Egyptian ship were found buried close to the pharaoh Khufu's tomb. It took over 13 years for the pieces to be reassembled into a 43.5-metre-long wooden ship.

2,000 gods and goddesses were worshipped by the ancient Egyptians. Some of these had animal heads, such as Anubis, the god of the dead and Horus, god of the sky.

700 small pictures called hieroglyphs made up the ancient Egyptian alphabet. They were all consonants and no vowels.

100,000 was shown in ancient Egyptian hieroglyphs by either a drawing of a frog or a tadpole.

100 was shown in ancient Egyptian hieroglyphs by a small drawing of a coil of rope.

70 days was the typical time it took to turn a dead body into a carefully preserved mummy, all wrapped up in linen strips and ready to be buried.

4-metre-long Nile crocodiles were one of the biggest dangers to ancient Egyptians fishing, bathing or washing clothes in the River Nile.

22 stone statues of baboons are found carved on the outside of the temple of Ramesses II at Abu Simbel. Sounds like some ancient Egyptians were monkey mad!

0 garments of clothing were worn by ancient Egyptian children, according to historians.

5,500 chariots were involved in the biggest chariot fight ever at the Battle of Kadesh around 3,300 years ago. The forces of Pharaoh Ramesses II battled with the Hittites in what is now Syria.

40 mummies were found buried together in Deir el Bahri in 1881, one of which was the great pharaoh, Ramesses II. When flown to Paris, France in 1974, he was issued with a passport which put his job as, king (deceased).

180,000 ancient Egyptian mummies of animals, mostly cats, were shipped from Egypt to Liverpool in the 1880s to be crushed up and spread on farm fields as fertilizer.

3 seasons divided up an ancient Egyptian year. Akhet was when the Nile flooded the farmlands; Peret was when crops were planted and grown and Shemu, from March to May, was when crops were harvested.

Bonkers Buildings

4.5 tonnes is the weight of an enormous crystal chandelier in Turkey's Dolmabahçe Palace. That's as heavy as an adult Asian elephant.

30 million mosaic tiles can be seen in a museum called Hagia Sofia, in Istanbul, Turkey.

4 different American states can be seen from the top of the Sears Tower in Chicago on a clear day.

7 man-made waterfalls can be found at a glamorous hotel called the Wynn Resort in Las Vegas, USA.

6,500 windows are found in the Empire State Building in New York, USA.

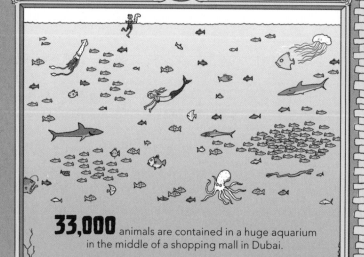

33,000 animals are contained in a huge aquarium in the middle of a shopping mall in Dubai.

4.2 metres is the length of the minute hand on a clock, commonly called Big Ben, in London, England.

40,000 lightbulbs are used in Buckingham Palace in London, England.

35,000 works of art are housed in the Louvre gallery in Paris, France.

1,056,006 tiles cover the roof of the Sydney Opera House in Australia.

410 days was all it took to build the Empire State Building in New York, USA.

102 is the number of floors in the Empire State Building.

20 per cent of all the trees in the city of Tokyo, Japan, can be found in the grounds of the Imperial Palace.

20,000 workers were employed to build a monument called the Taj Mahal in India.

28 different types of precious stone were used to build the Taj Mahal.

44 lifts can be found in the Shard – London's tallest skyscraper.

8,704 rooms can be found in the Forbidden City palaces in Beijing, China.

158 is the floor on which the world's highest mosque can be found, in Dubai's Burj Khalifa.

4 degrees is the angle at which the Leaning Tower of Pisa in Italy leans.

100,000 people gathered to watch a Frenchman called Alain Robert climb the National Bank of Abu Dhabi without any ropes or climbing equipment.

1,860 steps take you from street level to the top floor of the Empire State Building.

100 kilograms of gold cover the outside of the Golden Temple at Amritsar, India.

78 bathrooms can be found in Buckingham Palace, London, England.

50 tonnes of dark brown paint are used every 7 years to repaint the Eiffel Tower in Paris, France.

6,225 square metres of glass are contained in the Sydney Opera House, Australia.

1.5 hours is the time it can take to move 1 of the Sultan of Brunei's cars out of his garage, as it contains thousands of vehicles.

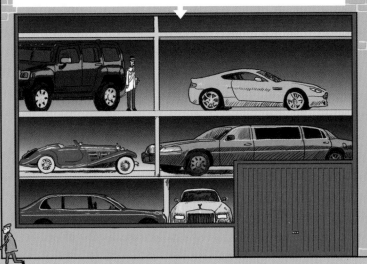

Battles and Armies

50,000 Romans were killed in a single battle called the Battle of Cannae in 216 BCE. They were defeated by the forces of a famous general named Hannibal.

450 bullets, known as rounds, could be fired each minute by a Lewis machine gun during World War I.

168 Spanish soldiers, called conquistadors, arrived in a city called Cajamarca in South America in 1532. They successfully battled and conquered the people who lived there, called Incas, whose armies numbered as many as 80,000.

300 metres was the distance that a type of catapult called a trebuchet could fling a rock during a castle siege.

42.195 kilometres is the distance that an ancient Greek messenger is said to have run in 490 BCE to spread the good news of a victory in battle. The battle took place in Marathon, and today this term is used for a race that is 42.195 kilometres long.

4.8 kilometres per hour was the top speed over ground of a very early tank called Little Willie. It was used by British forces in World War I.

3 pigeons were placed inside an experimental US missile in the 1940s. They were supposed to guide the missile by pecking on a screen. This bird-brained weapon was not a success.

120 kilograms was the weight of each shell fired by enormous Paris Guns during World War I.

2,285,000 men and women served in China's army and other military forces in 2011.

70 cities, and possibly even more than this, were founded by a famous general called Alexander the Great as he led his army of more than 30,000 men on conquests in Europe, Africa and Asia.

1,357,800 French soldiers were killed during World War I.

10–12 arrows could be fired in a single minute by a skilled longbowman in medieval times.

2 French regiments during the Battle of Fleurus in 1690 mistook each other for the enemy and attacked each other. Oops!

1 in **10** Roman soldiers would be killed by a punishment called decimation. If an army unit made a mistake, 1 soldier would be punished and sometimes executed.

54 cents was the cost of a paint scraper that was dropped and got jammed inside a US Navy submarine called the *Swordfish*, in 1978. It cost $171,000 to repair the submarine.

3 weeks before fighting the Normans at the Battle of Hastings (1066), King Harold's army had been in the north of England fighting the Vikings at the Battle of Stamford Bridge.

80 aircraft were shot down by World War I's most successful fighter pilot – a man called Manfred von Richthofen.

51,112 soldiers are believed to have been killed or injured at the Battle of Gettysburg (1863). This made it the deadliest battle of the American Civil War.

5 seconds was all a soldier had to throw a No.74 (ST) grenade before it exploded. Designed with a covering that would stick to enemy vehicles, the World War II grenade often got stuck to the thrower's clothing.

250 women are estimated to have disguised themselves as men to fight in the American Civil War of 1861–1865.

1.2 metres was the length of a type of sword carried by Aztec warriors in Mexico called a Macuahuitl. Sharp pieces of stone were inserted along the edges of the sword, making it a lethal weapon.

60 per cent of all British officers involved at the start of a battle in World War I called the Battle of the Somme died on the first day of fighting.

0 soldiers are in Costa Rica's army. The laws of this central American country have forbidden it from having a permanent army since 1949.

110 people make up the world's smallest army. This is the Swiss Guard that is the protection force for Vatican City, where the Pope lives.

21 years was the length of the Siege of Candia (1648–69) in Crete. It is considered to be the longest siege in history.

5 different types of cannon were on board a 16th-century Korean warship known as a turtle ship. The iron-clad boat had a dragon head at the front that could shoot flames to scare enemies.

22,717 casualties occurred in a single day of fighting during the Battle of Antietam – the bloodiest battle of the American Civil War.

Stars and Planets

3 Earths would fit inside a giant storm on Jupiter, called the Great Red Spot.

164.8 Earth years equal 1 Neptune year – the time it takes the planet Neptune to complete an orbit around the Sun. So Neptune is not great for birthdays.

27 moons orbit around the planet Uranus.

75.3 years pass between every visit of Halley's Comet to the Earth's night sky. The next time the comet can be spotted from the Earth will be in 2061.

299,792 kilometres per second is the speed that light travels through the Universe from stars such as our Sun.

25 kilometres is the height of a volcano called Olympus Mons on Mars. It's 2.5 times the height of Mount Everest, making it the tallest mountain in the entire Solar System.

464 degrees Celsius is the surface temperature of Venus – scorching! The metals tin, zinc and lead would all melt on the planet's surface.

3 billion kilometres is the approximate diameter of VY Canis Majoris. It's one of the largest stars in the Universe and more than 2,000 times bigger than the Sun.

4,000 kilometres is the length of a giant canyon called Valles Marineris on Mars. It is 7 kilometres deep in places – 5 times deeper than the Grand Canyon in the USA.

317.8 planet Earths would be needed to match the mass of Jupiter, the largest planet in the Solar System.

6 million times is how much brighter the distant star Cygnus OB2-12 shines than our Sun.

1 planet in the Solar System – Saturn – is less dense than water and would float in a swimming pool (if a big enough one could be found).

10-year-old Kathryn Aurora Gray was the youngest person to discover a new supernova (an exploding star) in 2011.

43,000 kilometres an hour is the speed at which the giant planet Jupiter rotates. Despite being much bigger than the Earth, it completes a full rotation in under 10 hours.

5 pounds was the present given to 11-year-old Venetia Burney in 1930 when her suggestion for the name of a newly discovered planet was chosen. She named it Pluto. It is now known as a dwarf planet.

200 billion stars can be found in the Milky Way, the galaxy that contains the Earth.

167,000 is the diameter in kilometres of the smallest star, only 16 per cent bigger than Jupiter, discovered in 2004 and called Ogle-TR-122b.

26.8 kilometres is the diameter of Mars' largest moon, called Phobos. That's pretty tiny! The Earth's moon is 3,476 kilometres in diameter.

67 is the number of moons which orbit around the Solar System's largest planet, Jupiter.

29.5 is the number of years it takes Saturn to complete an orbit around the Sun.

716 is the number of times per second that a pulsar (a spinning star) called PSR J1748-2446ad spins round. That'll make you dizzy!

56 million years would be the length of a journey in a car travelling at 80 kilometres per hour from the Earth to Proxima Centauri, the nearest star outside the Solar System.

100,000 years would be needed for light to travel from one edge of the Milky Way to the other.

42 years is the length of a winter or summer on Uranus.

90 is the temperature in degrees Celsius of the coolest star found in the Universe so far, a star around 75 light years (the distance that light travels in 75 years) from the Earth. Most stars have a temperature of thousands of degrees.

1 single teaspoon of a dense white dwarf star would weigh 5–15 tonnes.

13 moons orbit around Neptune.

23 new moons were discovered orbiting Jupiter in the year 2003. Nice work, astronomers!

120 kilometres per second is the speed at which the Milky Way and Andromeda galaxies are moving towards each other on a possible collision course.

3.3 years is all the time Encke's Comet needs to complete its orbit around the Sun. Comets have cores 10–100 kilometres wide but their tails can be more than 100 million kilometres long.

250 million kilometres is the estimated length of the tail of the Great Comet seen in 1843. That's further than from the Earth to Mars.

Barmy Bugs

205 grams is the weight that a Megasoma beetle grub (the name for a baby beetle) can reach.

80 per cent of human deaths in Africa are from malaria, a disease passed on by mosquito bites.

62,760 times a minute is the record for the fastest insect wing beat, made by a tiny kind of midge.

1,417 different types of insects and other bugs are regularly eaten by people around the world.

70 centimetres is the height a 0.6-centimetre bug called a froghopper can leap. If you could jump that many times your own height, you'd clear a 250-metre building in 1 bound.

8 eyes are arranged in 4 pairs around the top of most spiders' heads.

3.5 trillion locusts were seen in a single swarm in Nebraska in 1875. The swarm covered 512,817 square kilometres.

55 metres was the length of a boot lace worm found washed up on the beach in Scotland in 1864. The whopping worm was more than twice as long as a cricket pitch.

30 species of spiders have strong enough venom to be really dangerous to people. Almost all of the world's 40,000 species of spider have a venomous bite.

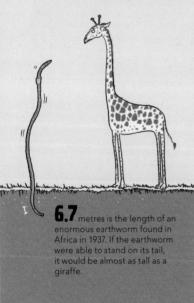

6.7 metres is the length of an enormous earthworm found in Africa in 1937. If the earthworm were able to stand on its tail, it would be almost as tall as a giraffe.

3 days is the length of time that the larvae of a type of midge can survive in liquid nitrogen – a chemical with a temperature of –196 degrees Celsius.

900 grams is the weight of the biggest recorded African giant snail. This super-snail was 39.3 centimetres long.

75 centimetres was the wing span of an ancient kind of dragonfly that lived before the dinosaurs.

30,000 eggs are laid by some queen termites every day.

300 million years ago, the first cockroaches were scuttling around in North America.

30 centimetres is the leg span of the biggest huntsman spiders in the world.

750 legs is the record for any animal in the world. This leggy beast is a rare American millipede, whose scientific name means full of legs.

3,432 kilometres were covered by 1 migrating monarch butterfly on its journey south. It was fitted with a satellite tag so its journey could be tracked.

11 kilometres is the distance over which a male emperor moth can smell a female.

58 kilometres an hour is the top flying speed of the Australian dragonfly, the fastest-flying insect in the world.

30 metres of silk can be churned out by 1 spider every day.

5,000 insects can be eaten by a single ladybird in its lifetime.

12.8 metres was the height of a huge termite mound found in Africa. That's the same height as a 4-storey building.

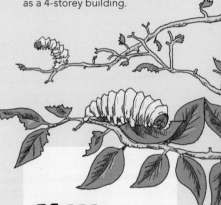

71 grams is the weight of the heaviest ever adult insect, a giant weta from New Zealand. The giant weta weighs the same as 3 mice.

1.5 metres is the circumference of a golden orb-web spider's web.

400,000 different species of beetles are known to science. Of all the known animal species alive on Earth today, 1 in every 4 is a kind of beetle.

86,000 times its own body weight in leaves is eaten by a polyphemus moth caterpillar in its first 56 days of life.

150 silkworm cocoons are needed to supply enough silk to make a silk tie.

100 metres long and 1 metre wide, a marching column of army ants may be made up of more than 1 million individual ants.

511 earthworms were charmed out of the ground in just 30 minutes, by a schoolboy named Tom Shufflebotham. He enticed the worms to come to the surface by jiggling a pitchfork in the soil.

North America

6,194 metres is the height of Alaska's Mount McKinley, the highest mountain in North America.

50 states make up the country of the United States of America. Hawaii was the last state to join in 1959.

200,000 alligators live in the Florida Everglades.

90 per cent of Jamaica's population is of African descent, despite the fact that Jamaica lies in the Caribbean Sea.

23 countries make up the continent of North America. These are: Canada, the USA, Antigua, the Bahamas, Barbados, Jamaica, Haiti, Dominica, the Dominican Republic, Trinidad and Tobago, St Kitts and Nevis, St Lucia, St Vincent and the Grenadines, Cuba, Grenada, Panama, Belize, Costa Rica, El Salvador, Honduras, Guatemala, Mexico and Nicaragua. The island of Greenland is also in North America but forms part of the kingdom of Denmark.

269 square kilometres is the size of St Kitts and Nevis, the smallest North American country.

42 volcanoes can be found in Mexico. Many of them are still active.

75 per cent of the world's geysers (hot springs) can be found in Yellowstone National Park in the USA.

24,230,000 square kilometres is the area of the continent of North America.

4,088 kilometres is the length of the Missouri, the longest river in North America.

7.2 million dollars was the price the USA paid Russia when it purchased Alaska.

446 kilometres is the length of the Grand Canyon in Arizona. It is up to 1,800 metres deep and is one of the most spectacular natural wonders of the world.

21 per cent of the entire world's supply of fresh water is contained in the Great Lakes in the USA and Canada. These are Lakes Superior, Michigan, Huron, Erie and Ontario.

80,000 people were needed to dig the Panama Canal, which links the Atlantic and Pacific Oceans. It reduces the journey between the 2 oceans from over 12,880 kilometres around South America to just the 30-kilometre length of the canal.

4.8 per cent of the planet's surface is taken up by North America.

209 native American languages are still spoken in the USA and Canada, along with many more in Central America and Mexico.

13 stripes and **50** stars are on the flag of the USA. These represent the original 13 states and the current 50 states.

4,800 kilometres is the length of the Rocky Mountain range, which stretches from Canada in the north to New Mexico in the southern USA.

98 per cent of the Caribbean's islands are uninhabited.

2 official languages are recognized in Canada: English and French. Nearly 1 in 5 of the population can speak both languages.

40 billion burgers are eaten each year in America.

7,000 islands and reefs are found in the Caribbean Sea.

2 million lakes are scattered throughout Canada. They contain enough water to cover the whole country to a depth of 2 metres.

40 per cent of the world's corn is grown in the USA.

20 metres high, the cardon is the largest cactus species in the world. It is found in the deserts of northern Mexico and the southern USA and can live for 200 years.

4 presidents of the United States are carved into the side of Mount Rushmore in South Dakota, USA. These are George Washington, Thomas Jefferson, Theodore Roosevelt and Abraham Lincoln.

Dinosaurs

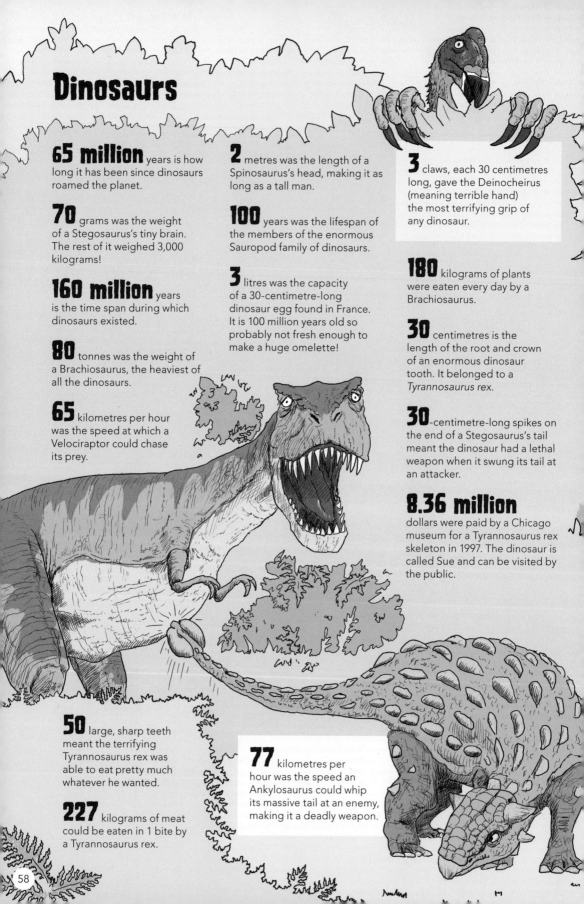

65 million years is how long it has been since dinosaurs roamed the planet.

70 grams was the weight of a Stegosaurus's tiny brain. The rest of it weighed 3,000 kilograms!

160 million years is the time span during which dinosaurs existed.

80 tonnes was the weight of a Brachiosaurus, the heaviest of all the dinosaurs.

65 kilometres per hour was the speed at which a Velociraptor could chase its prey.

2 metres was the length of a Spinosaurus's head, making it as long as a tall man.

100 years was the lifespan of the members of the enormous Sauropod family of dinosaurs.

3 litres was the capacity of a 30-centimetre-long dinosaur egg found in France. It is 100 million years old so probably not fresh enough to make a huge omelette!

3 claws, each 30 centimetres long, gave the Deinocheirus (meaning terrible hand) the most terrifying grip of any dinosaur.

180 kilograms of plants were eaten every day by a Brachiosaurus.

30 centimetres is the length of the root and crown of an enormous dinosaur tooth. It belonged to a *Tyrannosaurus rex*.

30-centimetre-long spikes on the end of a Stegosaurus's tail meant the dinosaur had a lethal weapon when it swung its tail at an attacker.

8.36 million dollars were paid by a Chicago museum for a Tyrannosaurus rex skeleton in 1997. The dinosaur is called Sue and can be visited by the public.

50 large, sharp teeth meant the terrifying Tyrannosaurus rex was able to eat pretty much whatever he wanted.

227 kilograms of meat could be eaten in 1 bite by a Tyrannosaurus rex.

77 kilometres per hour was the speed an Ankylosaurus could whip its massive tail at an enemy, making it a deadly weapon.

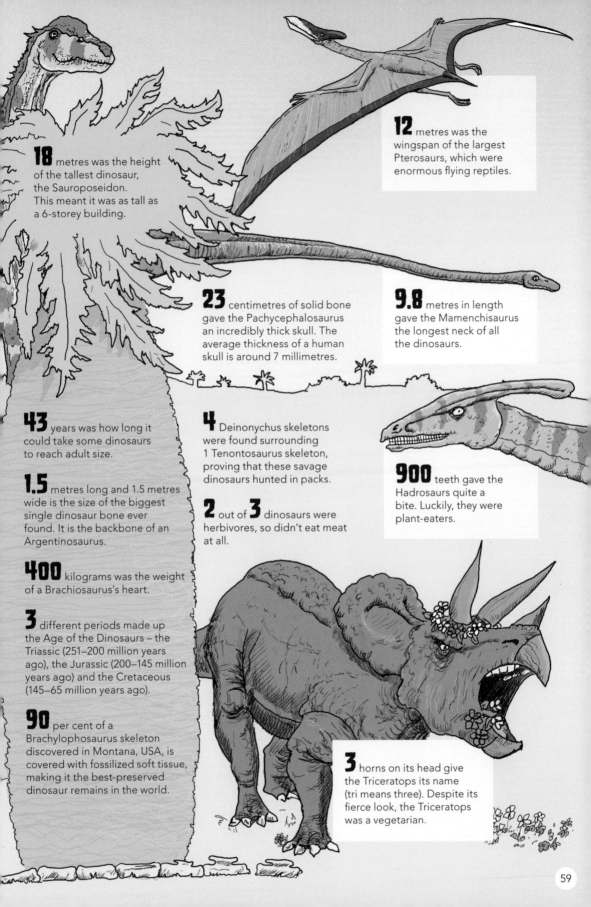

18 metres was the height of the tallest dinosaur, the Sauroposeidon. This meant it was as tall as a 6-storey building.

12 metres was the wingspan of the largest Pterosaurs, which were enormous flying reptiles.

23 centimetres of solid bone gave the Pachycephalosaurus an incredibly thick skull. The average thickness of a human skull is around 7 millimetres.

9.8 metres in length gave the Mamenchisaurus the longest neck of all the dinosaurs.

43 years was how long it could take some dinosaurs to reach adult size.

4 Deinonychus skeletons were found surrounding 1 Tenontosaurus skeleton, proving that these savage dinosaurs hunted in packs.

1.5 metres long and 1.5 metres wide is the size of the biggest single dinosaur bone ever found. It is the backbone of an Argentinosaurus.

900 teeth gave the Hadrosaurs quite a bite. Luckily, they were plant-eaters.

2 out of **3** dinosaurs were herbivores, so didn't eat meat at all.

400 kilograms was the weight of a Brachiosaurus's heart.

3 different periods made up the Age of the Dinosaurs – the Triassic (251–200 million years ago), the Jurassic (200–145 million years ago) and the Cretaceous (145–65 million years ago).

90 per cent of a Brachylophosaurus skeleton discovered in Montana, USA, is covered with fossilized soft tissue, making it the best-preserved dinosaur remains in the world.

3 horns on its head give the Triceratops its name (tri means three). Despite its fierce look, the Triceratops was a vegetarian.

Fabulous Fashion

7.5 centimetres was the length of Chinese girls' feet when they were bound, in a practice called Lotus Feet. The bones in their feet were broken and their feet were tied up. This was banned in 1949.

1,060 pairs of shoes were left behind by Imelda Marcos, the wife of a Philippine president, when she and her husband were sent away from their country.

450 million pairs of jeans are sold in the USA each year.

70,000 images can be shot by a single photographer during New York Fashion Week.

16 pairs of gloves were worn at the same time by a prince called Philip of Calabria, because he loved them so much!

2.69 kilometres was the length of a huge catwalk built in Ankara, Turkey.

642 rubies encrusted a glittering pair of shoes made by a designer called Stuart Weitzman.

2 kilometres was the length of the train on a very eccentric wedding dress!

3,500 pairs of ballet shoes are worn out by the ballerinas in the British Royal Ballet every year.

76-centimetre-high platform shoes, called Chopines, were fashionable in Venice in the 16th century.

46 centimetres is the height of the world's tallest ever top hat, made in 1913.

65 different costumes were worn by an actress called Elizabeth Taylor in the film Cleopatra.

40 centimetre waists were in fashion in the 19th century, when women wore laced corsets. Now, waists are around 85 centimetres.

22 kilograms of real beef were used to create a dress for singer Lady Gaga in 2010. That's one heavy frock!

4.6 million dollars were paid at auction for a dress belonging to a famous 60s film star, called Marilyn Monroe.

4 cities in the world host internationally recognized fashion weeks – when designers show their new collections on the catwalk. These cities are New York, London, Milan and Paris.

2,700 sparkling diamonds decorated a bottle of perfume that cost 1 million dollars.

I HATE WEDDINGS!

50,000 roses had their petals scattered along the runway of a Gucci fashion show.

2,009 peacock feathers were stitched together to create a magnificent wedding dress in China.

Dreadful Death

834 million is the number of fairground rides, on average, you would have to take before, statistically speaking, you would have a fatal accident.

-196 degrees Celsius is the temperature a human body or brain is frozen to in cryonic suspension. This is when a body is preserved for a future time, when medical advances might be able to bring it back to life.

4 billion pounds was left to 2 penniless Hungarian brothers, Zsolt and Geza Peladi, by their grandmother in 2009. The brothers had been living in a cave and scavenging scraps to eat, before charity workers found them to give them the news.

30,000 dollars is the price of a deluxe coffin. It's made of solid bronze and covered in gold.

600 people die in the United States every year from falling out of bed.

200,000 pounds was left to the sons of a man called Henry Budd in 1862. The only condition was that they never grew moustaches.

23 times – this is how much more likely drivers are to end their journeys in a crash when they are texting.

1.4 metres was the length of Hans Steininger's beard in 1567. It was so long that he tripped over it, fell and died from a broken neck.

21 people drowned in Boston, USA in 1919, when a giant tank holding sticky molasses sugar broke, and a huge wave of molasses swept through the streets.

13 guns were fired by a ship called the *Jackal* in 1794 to salute an American explorer called John Kendrick. He was standing in his boat nearby, when a shot from one of the ship's guns hit and killed him. Whoops!

20 minutes after William Townley was hanged at Gloucester in 1811, a horseman arrived at the scene carrying a legal letter cancelling the death sentence.

11 axe strokes were needed to chop off the head of an English noblewoman called the Countess of Salisbury in 1541.

163 tonnes of junk, from old newspapers to broken prams, were found in two brothers' New York apartment after they died. One brother was killed when the rubbish fell on him and the other brother was trapped inside the apartment.

870–980 degrees Celsius is the temperature inside a cremation furnace chamber, known as a retort.

1,500 hours of work are required to plastinate a dead body. This means preserving the body by replacing some of its fluids with a liquid that's a lot like a plastic.

37 deaths occurred in the United States between 1978 and 1995 due to people rocking vending machines. The machines toppled on to them and killed them.

21,000 human skeletons can be found in a cellar below the Skull Chapel in Czermna, Poland. Hundreds of leg bones can be found built into the chapel's ceiling as well.

ELIZABETH ROSSETTI
1829–1862

7 years after burying his wife, a painter and poet called Dante Gabriel Rossetti opened up her coffin again. He wanted to retrieve the only copy of some of his poems that he had buried with her.

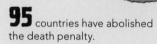

95 countries have abolished the death penalty.

2,427 people died when a giant avalanche hit a Swiss town called Plurs in 1618.

1 in **79,842** is the chance of dying from a bee, hornet or wasp sting in the United States.

9 people were killed after a brewery's tanks burst in London in 1814. The street was flooded with over 1 million litres of beer.

32 people were killed on board *HMS Trinidad* in 1942, when a torpedo it fired in battle proved to be faulty. It whizzed off in a large circle and returned to strike the ship.

29 years after an English explorer named Sir Walter Raleigh was beheaded, his wife still kept his head in a red leather bag.

Monster Machines

113 trailers were pulled by a single truck in 2006. Linked together, the truck and trailers made a vehicle over 1.47 kilometres long.

2.3 seconds is the time a Bugatti Veyron car takes to brake from 100 kilometres per hour to a standstill.

90 seconds or less is the time it takes the Terrafugia Transition® flying car to fold up its wings after landing and drive away like a regular motor vehicle.

202.9 kilometres per hour was the speed that a land vehicle called the Greenbird reached in 2009. It had no engine and was powered by winds across a dry lake in Nevada, USA.

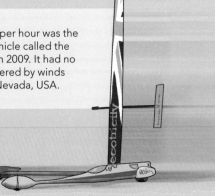

3 million US dollars is what it costs to buy the world's most expensive mobile home, known as an RV. It comes complete with a sun deck, fireplace and glow-in-the-dark paint so it won't be missed at night.

0.8 seconds is all it takes for a type of car made for drag racing, called a Top Fuel dragster, to accelerate from a standstill to 160 kilometres per hour.

266 kilometres per hour was the speed Billy Baxter reached whilst riding his motorbike in 2003. He became the fastest blind motorcyclist of all time.

18 litres of fuel were burned every second by the jet engines of a supersonic car called the Thrust SCC. It broke the world land speed record with a speed of 1,228 kilometres per hour.

85 aircraft can be found on board the giant USS *Nimitz* aircraft carrier.

6,318 passengers can travel on the world's biggest cruise liner, the RCI *Allure Of The Seas*. The liner is a whopping 362 metres long and includes a library, ice-skating rink and park area with over 12,000 plants.

890 kilograms of steel and 3,850 kilograms of rubber are found in a single 59/80R63 XDR tyre built for giant dump trucks. There's enough rubber in each tyre to make 600 regular car tyres.

38,000 cubic centimetres (cc) is the size of a giant engine used to power a huge 5.5-metre-long Harzer Bike Schmiede motorcycle with sidecar. Most family cars are only 1,200–2,200cc.

150,000 different measurements from the onboard computer in a Williams FW26 Formula One car are sent back to its race team's base every second while it's racing.

398 metres is the length of the Emma Maersk, a massive container cargo ship. That's longer than 4 football pitches.

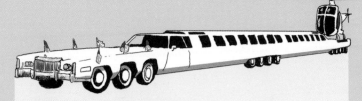

61.57 metres was the length a monster truck jumped when it drove up a ramp and leapt over a Boeing 727 airliner in 1999. What a stunt!

50 cars can be carried by an enormous cargo plane, the Antonov AN-225 Mriya. The aircraft can carry cargos weighing as much as 250 tonnes.

1,088 kilograms is the weight of each 3.04-metre-high tyre on a Bigfoot 5 monster truck. Each of those tyres is heavier than 2 adult horses.

418 passengers and up to 60 cars could be carried by the world's largest civilian hovercraft, the SR.N4, which operated across the English Channel from 1968 to 2000.

26 wheels are found on the world's longest stretch limousine car. It measures more than 30 metres in length and has a sun deck, jacuzzi and helicopter landing pad.

85 tonnes of rock or earth can be scooped up in a single go by a construction vehicle called the Terex RH 400 excavator – that's more than the weight of 20 hippos.

22 tonnes of ice, containing the preserved body of an extinct woolly mammoth, were lifted into the air and carried to a lab by a powerful Mil Mi-26 helicopter in 1999.

0.06 seconds is all that it takes for an airbag on a Honda Goldwing GL1800 motorcycle to detect a crash and inflate with nitrogen gas to protect the rider's head.

120 degrees Celsius is the temperature that a Formula One car's tyres reach after a race – hot enough to fry an egg on.

475.8 litres of fuel is used by a vehicle called the Space Shuttle crawler transporter for every 1.6 kilometres it carries the Shuttle to its launchpad.

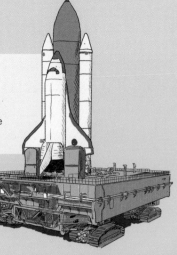

605 kilometres per hour is the maximum speed of the Shockwave – a large truck powered by 3 aircraft jet engines.

853 passengers can fly in a single airliner, the enormous Airbus A380.

Dangerous Animals

471 people are known to have been killed by sharks since 1580. Another 1,992 people have survived shark attacks.

1.8 metres is the height of a cassowary, an Australian bird that, when angry, can kick a person to death.

800 people a year die from snakebites in Sri Lanka, making this the riskiest country in the world, snakewise.

10–15 surfers are bitten by sharks each year at New Smyrna Beach, Florida, USA.

1 species of wild bird, the African crowned eagle, is suspected of hunting humans on occasion. The remains of very young children have been found around its nest.

2.25 metres is the average length of a male Komodo dragon, the world's biggest lizard and the only one that makes a habit of eating humans.

7 out of **23** species of crocodiles and their relatives are known to have eaten people.

750,000 stinging organs are on each of the 30-metre tentacles of a Portuguese man o' war – a jellyfish-like animal. The stings are incredibly painful but rarely fatal.

1,600 kilograms is the estimated bite force of a great white shark.

1 person is known to have been killed by a leopard seal, the fiercest of all the seals.

600 milligrams of venom, carried by a large gaboon viper, is enough to kill 10 adult humans.

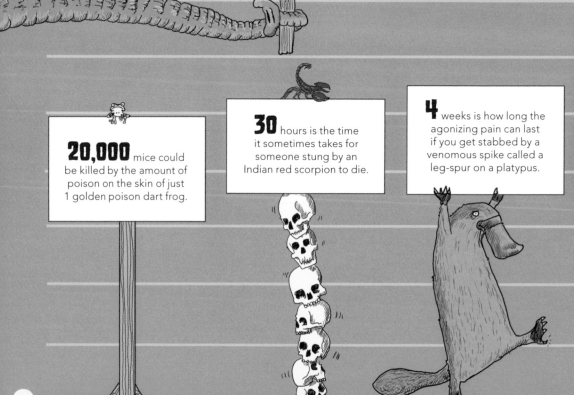

500 people are killed by elephants each year, usually by being trampled.

20,000 mice could be killed by the amount of poison on the skin of just 1 golden poison dart frog.

30 hours is the time it sometimes takes for someone stung by an Indian red scorpion to die.

4 weeks is how long the agonizing pain can last if you get stabbed by a venomous spike called a leg-spur on a platypus.

2 metres is the distance over which a spitting cobra can spit venom from its fangs. It aims for its victim's eyes and can cause blindness.

10 centimetres is the average length of a geographer cone, a deadly sea-snail that fires venom-laden darts through a hole in the tip of its shell.

300 people a year, on average, are killed by angry hippos. The hippo is the most dangerous large animal in Africa.

19 kilometres an hour is the top slithering speed for a highly venomous black mamba. This makes the speedy snake tricky to run away from.

1.35 milligrams of venom are carried in a wandering spider's 1-centimetre-long venom glands.

14 human deaths from redback spider bites have been recorded in Australia, but none since 1956 when an antivenom was developed.

2.5 million people are bitten by snakes worldwide every year, 125,000 of them fatally.

650 volts of electricity can be generated by a large electric eel – that's enough to kill a person.

10 centimetres is the size of a blue-ringed octopus, but it has enough venom to kill 10 people.

3 species of pitohui birds from New Guinea are poisonous and will make you ill if you eat them.

700 kilograms is the weight of a massive African Cape buffalo. These animals are so large and intimidating that even lions avoid trying to hunt them.

462 stitches were needed by a fisherman called Rodney Fox after he was bitten by a great white shark in 1963.

300 people were eaten by piranhas in a single day in 1981 when their boat capsized in Brazil.

3 people, on average, are killed each year by wild bears in the USA and Canada.

20 minutes is how long it would take you to die if you ate the poisonous parts of a fugu puffer fish. This fish is a delicacy in Japan, where trained chefs are expert at removing the deadly bits, leaving just the delicious bits.

4 joggers were attacked and clawed by an angry buzzard in Fife, Scotland, in 2009.

The Romans

BURN, BABY, BURN!

6 days of horror gripped Rome in CE 64 as fire raged through the city, destroying much of it. Legend has it that the fire was started by the Emperor Nero himself.

1 person in the entire Roman Empire was allowed to wear a purple toga – the Emperor. Lesser nobles were sometimes allowed to have a purple stripe on theirs.

7 letters were used to represent numbers in ancient Rome. These were I (1), V (5), X (10), L (50), C (100), D (500) and M (1000), and they could be combined to make other numbers.

6.5 million square kilometres was the area of land covered by the Roman Empire at its largest.

45 metres is the height of Monte Testaccio, a hill made entirely of millions of broken ceramic jars called amphorae and used by the Romans for storing food and drink. The hill is an enormous Roman rubbish tip.

2 brothers – Romulus and Remus – founded Rome in 753 BCE. The legend of the twins tells us that the boys were raised by a wolf.

3 metres of cloth were used for a toga – the tunic worn by the Romans.

25 per cent of the population of ancient Rome were slaves.

6,000 slaves were executed as punishment for the famous slave revolt led by a gladiator called Spartacus.

7 hills make up the Hills of Rome. These are the Aventine, Caelian, Capitoline, Esquiline, Palatine, Quirinal and Viminal Hills.

60 million people lived in the Roman Empire at its peak.

3 heads belonged to Cerberus, the dog from Roman and Greek myth who guarded the entrance to the underworld. It was his job to make sure no one left.

GRRR!

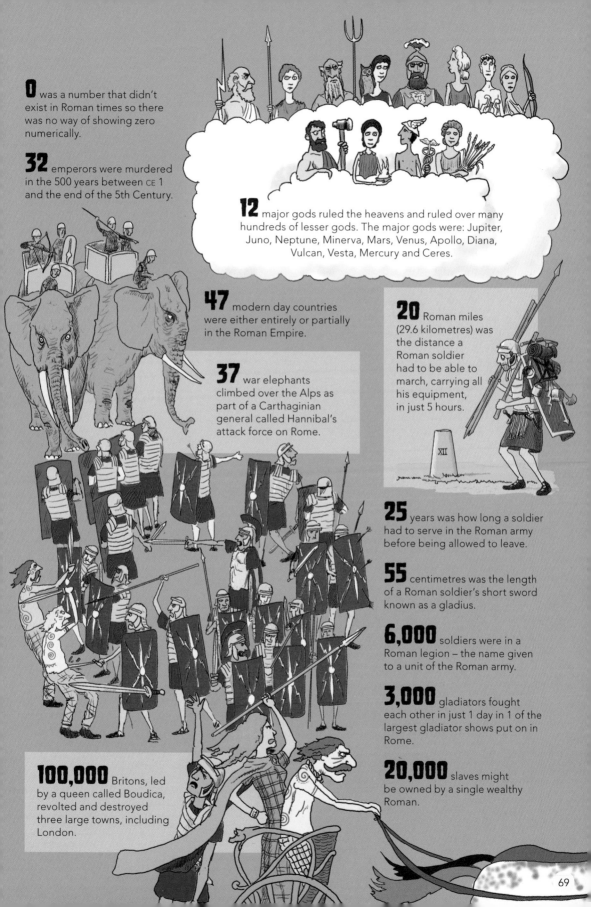

0 was a number that didn't exist in Roman times so there was no way of showing zero numerically.

32 emperors were murdered in the 500 years between CE 1 and the end of the 5th Century.

12 major gods ruled the heavens and ruled over many hundreds of lesser gods. The major gods were: Jupiter, Juno, Neptune, Minerva, Mars, Venus, Apollo, Diana, Vulcan, Vesta, Mercury and Ceres.

47 modern day countries were either entirely or partially in the Roman Empire.

20 Roman miles (29.6 kilometres) was the distance a Roman soldier had to be able to march, carrying all his equipment, in just 5 hours.

37 war elephants climbed over the Alps as part of a Carthaginian general called Hannibal's attack force on Rome.

25 years was how long a soldier had to serve in the Roman army before being allowed to leave.

55 centimetres was the length of a Roman soldier's short sword known as a gladius.

6,000 soldiers were in a Roman legion – the name given to a unit of the Roman army.

3,000 gladiators fought each other in just 1 day in 1 of the largest gladiator shows put on in Rome.

100,000 Britons, led by a queen called Boudica, revolted and destroyed three large towns, including London.

20,000 slaves might be owned by a single wealthy Roman.

Amazing Adventures

12 chocolate milkshakes were all that Steve Fossett had for food as he flew a plane called the Virgin Atlantic GlobalFlyer around the world in 2005. The journey took 67 hours and was the first ever non-stop, solo, unrefuelled, round-the-world flight by an aircraft.

69 was the number of days a diver called Richard Presley spent living underwater in a module off the coast of Florida in 1992.

321 metres is the drop on the world's highest bungee jump, from the Royal Gorge Bridge in Colorado, USA. Not for the faint-hearted!

15 piranhas a day were eaten by Ed Stafford as he completed an epic walk of more than 6,500 kilometres along the entire length of the Amazon river in 2008.

250 metres was the height reached by the first ever balloon ascent over Antarctica, made in 1902 by a famous polar explorer called Robert Falcon Scott. The balloon, which was tethered to the ground, was named Eva and was filled with hydrogen gas.

63-year-old schoolteacher, Annie Edson Taylor, became the first person to survive a trip over Niagara Falls in 1901. She rode the giant waterfall crammed inside a wooden barrel.

53 pairs of trainers were worn out by Rosie Swale-Pope during an epic run around the world. It took her 1,789 days to complete the trip, which started on her 57th birthday.

1,342 kilometres per hour was the top speed that fearless Felix Baumgartner reached when jumping out of a balloon 39,000 metres above the ground in 2012. Felix opened his parachute just 2,516 metres from the ground.

1,162 sand dunes were travelled over by Pat Farmer as he crossed Australia's Simpson Desert. He covered 379 kilometres in 3⅓ days, in scorching temperatures.

14 buses were jumped by a famous daredevil known as Evel Knievel riding a motorcycle in Ohio, USA in 1975.

DRAT! I FORGOT THE PEPPER ...

14 mountains on Earth have peaks above 8,000 metres. Climbing these 'eight thousanders' is a goal of all serious mountain climbers.

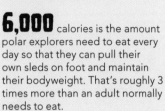

6,000 calories is the amount polar explorers need to eat every day so that they can pull their own sleds on foot and maintain their bodyweight. That's roughly 3 times more than an adult normally needs to eat.

5 centimetres was the width of a rope along which Charles Blondin tightrope-walked to cross Niagara Falls in 1859. Three years later, Blondin cooked an omelette while standing on a rope above Niagara Falls. What a thrill-seeker!

76-year-old Min Bahadur Sherchan from Nepal became the oldest person to climb Mount Everest when he reached the summit in May 2008.

21 is the number of times a climber called Apa Sherpa, has reached the peak of Mount Everest.

13-year-old Jordan Romero reached the summit of Mount Everest – the tallest mountain in the world – in 2010.

72 days was all Nellie Bly (real name: Elizabeth Jane Cochran) needed to become the fastest round-the-world traveller in 1889. Cochran used steamships and railways to travel over 39,500 kilometres. She met Jules Verne – the author of *Around The World In 80 Days* – in France along the way.

272 litres of rum was just 1 of the hundreds of items that 2 explorers called Burke and Wills carried on their 1860–61 expedition across Australia. The rum wasn't for them, however, it was for their camels!

1,305 minutes is the time it took for Matthew Webb to become the first person to swim the English Channel (between England and France) in 1875.

270 men set out on a round-the-world voyage in 1519, led by Ferdinand Magellan. Only 18 completed the journey.

3,565 kilograms of a type of fermented cabbage called sauerkraut was carried on board Captain Cook's ship, *HMS Endeavour* for his first voyage across the Pacific ocean.

13,790 kilometres was the distance paddled by Freya Hoffmeister as she travelled around the entire coast of Australia in a kayak. She had to contend with saltwater crocodiles and sharks, one of which bit two holes in her boat.

Arctic and Antarctic

6 weeks is the length of time the north Greenland village of Illulissat spends in total darkness in the Arctic winter where the Sun never rises above the horizon.

-52 degrees Celsius is the bone-chilling temperature that has to be reached before the school in the Russian town of Oymyakon will close. Up until 2008, schoolchildren in this cold Russian town had to use an outside toilet. Brrr!

4 million people live within the Arctic Circle.

19 metres per day is the speed at which the ice in the Sermeq Kujalleq glacier in Greenland moves.

307,700 is the population of the Russian city of Murmansk, the largest settlement inside the Arctic Circle.

14 years is how long it takes the woolly bear caterpillar, which lives in the Arctic, to finally become a moth. It freezes solid every winter, then thaws again in the summer to feed.

240 days of the year, the Aurora Borealis, also known as the Northern lights, can be seen in Yellowknife, Canada.

North Pole

30 guests joined explorer Borge Ousland and his fiancée, Hege, as they became the first couple to marry at the North Pole in 2012. The weather on the day was sunny but the temperature was -23 degrees Celsius.

20,000-25,000 polar bears are estimated to roam wild in the Arctic. They live for up to 25 years in the wild.

3 metres is the length of the giant pointed tusk on a narwhal's head. Narwhals live in the waters of the Arctic.

58 is the number of times the United Kingdom would fit into Antarctica.

1,100 people visit and stay at the McMurdo Station, the largest science base on Antarctica, during the summer. The station lies about 1,350 kilometres from the South Pole.

26.5 million cubic kilometres is the amount of ice on Antarctica.

1 is the number of working cash machines on Antarctica. The single machine, which gives out as much as $50,000 in a week, is found at the McMurdo Station – a scientific base.

70 per cent of the entire planet's fresh water is found in Antarctica.

37,800 tourists visited Antarctica in 2009 on large ships. 26,000 landed on the Antarctic continent itself.

7 millimetres is the length of the largest animal to spend all its time on land in Antarctica. It's a type of insect called *Belgica antarctica*.

1,267 people spent the whole of the bitter Antarctic winter at the South Pole between 1957 and 2009.

23 is the number of airports or air strips on Antarctica. There are also 53 helipads.

20,000 meteorites (rocks from space) have been found in Antarctica.

303 hours (just under 13 days) is the record for crossing Antarctica set in 2010. The team travelled 1,946 kilometres using monster trucks.

500 billion tonnes of ice floated off into the Southern Ocean when the Larsen B ice shelf broke away from Antarctica in 2002.

70,900 kilometres is the distance that a bird called the Arctic tern flies on its migration journeys from the Arctic to Antarctica and back again each year.

5 million is the approximate number of penguins found in and around Antarctica. The largest species, the emperor penguin, can weigh up to 40 kilograms.

South Pole

4 species of penguin live and breed on Antarctica – the Adélie, gentoo, emperor and chinstrap penguin. No penguins live in the Arctic.

52 Greenland husky dogs were used to pull the 4 sleds used by a Norwegian explorer called Roald Amundsen when his party became the first to reach the South Pole on December 14th, 1911.

565 metres is the maximum depth an emperor penguin can dive underwater to feed. Emperor penguins can stay underwater for over 20 minutes.

Fish and Sealife

90 years is the lifespan of some sea anemones.

7.9 millimetres is the size of a tiny Asian swamp fish called *Paedocrypsis progenetica* – its name is longer than its body.

400 metres of airspace can be covered by a flying fish in its gliding flight through the air.

60 adult humans could be killed by the venom of just 1 box jellyfish.

250 million herring can team up to form a mega-shoal.

100 years is the time it takes a deep-sea clam to grow to just 8 millimetres in size.

6 milliseconds is all it takes for a frogfish to catch its prey. It does this by opening its jaws wide at lightning speed, and sucking its dinner in.

30 centimetres of coral is eaten by a crown-of-thorns starfish every day.

32,000 species of fish are known to science, so far. That's 6 species of fish for every 1 species of mammal.

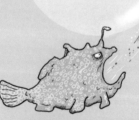

3 metres is the length of the tail fin of a 6-metre-long thresher shark.

70 million years is the age of the most recent fossils of coelacanth fish. These deep-sea fish were thought to be extinct but were then found alive and well in 1938.

12.65 metres is the length of an enormous whale shark caught off the coast of Pakistan. That's larger than some boats.

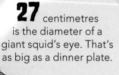

27 centimetres is the diameter of a giant squid's eye. That's as big as a dinner plate.

405 years is the estimated age of a quahog clam that was uprooted from the seabed off Iceland in 2007.

109 kilometres an hour is the top swimming speed of a sailfish. That's about the same speed as a car driving on a motorway.

8 litres of slime can be produced by a hagfish in just a few minutes. They use this sticky goo to clog up the gills of their predators, which allows them to escape.

1 metre is the length a walrus's tusks can grow to.

20,557 kilometres was covered by a leatherback sea turtle in 647 days, according to a satellite tag fitted to her shell.

1 year is how long it takes some starfish to regrow their arms if they are broken off.

291,000 different kinds of sea animals and plants have been discovered, but scientists think there may be another 750,000 more down there.

43.7 million red crabs migrate across Christmas Island in the Indian Ocean to the sea to breed every 5 years or so, bringing the 135-square kilometre island to a standstill.

205 years is the potential lifespan of the rougheye rockfish.

200 million years ago, horseshoe crabs looked much the same as they do today – it's no wonder they are called living fossils.

8,700 kilometres is the distance that humpback whales migrate. They are travelling from breeding grounds to feeding grounds, so they make this huge journey on an empty stomach.

2,388 metres is a record-breaking deep dive made by an elephant seal.

15 months is the length of time a swell shark can survive without eating.

200 arms grow on some feather starfish, with new arms forking out from old ones.

60 spiny lobsters migrate in a large group. They march single file along the seabed in one long line.

12 million is the approximate world population of crabeater seals. There are more of them in the world than any other large mammal – except humans.

20 metres across is the width of a small pool in Nevada, USA. It is the only place in the world where the devil's hole pupfish lives.

The Human Body

1.5 litres of fluid are produced every day by glands in your mouth called salivary glands.

1 litre is the amount of snot that you swallow every day. Yuck!

0.1 centimetres is the length of the smallest muscle in your body. It's found in your ear.

1.3 kilograms is the weight of an average human brain.

2 is the number of times around the world your blood vessels would stretch if they were laid out in a line.

12 days is all it takes for your tongue to grow a whole new set of taste buds.

5 months is the average amount of time your eyelashes last for, before they fall out.

10,000 different smells can be picked out by your super-sensitive nose.

17 muscles in your face are used every time you smile.

8,000-9,000 litres of air are breathed in by your lungs every single day.

600,000 particles are shed by your skin every hour.

8 seconds is all it takes for food to travel from your mouth to your stomach.

100 billion nerve cells are in your brain, helping you to form thoughts, and making sure your body functions properly.

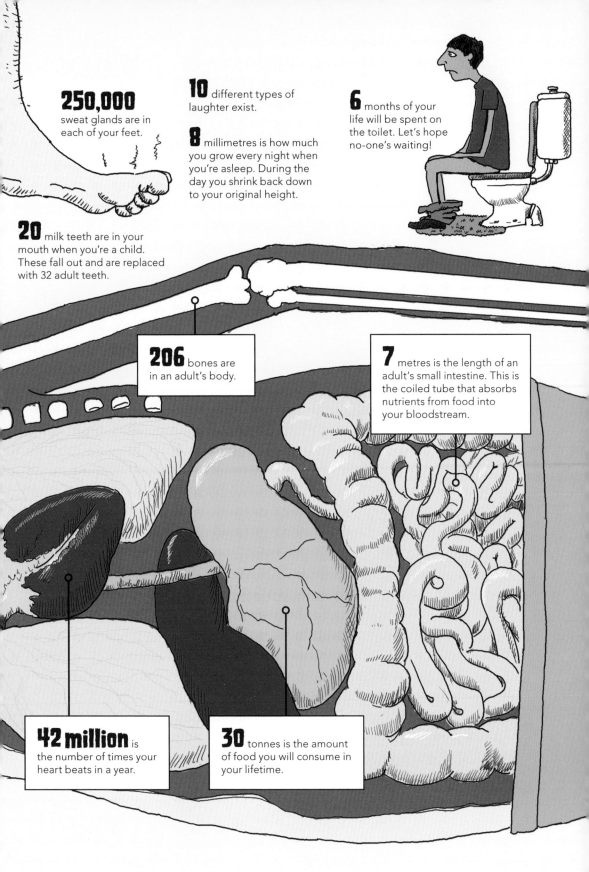

250,000 sweat glands are in each of your feet.

10 different types of laughter exist.

8 millimetres is how much you grow every night when you're asleep. During the day you shrink back down to your original height.

6 months of your life will be spent on the toilet. Let's hope no-one's waiting!

20 milk teeth are in your mouth when you're a child. These fall out and are replaced with 32 adult teeth.

206 bones are in an adult's body.

7 metres is the length of an adult's small intestine. This is the coiled tube that absorbs nutrients from food into your bloodstream.

42 million is the number of times your heart beats in a year.

30 tonnes is the amount of food you will consume in your lifetime.

Beautiful Birds

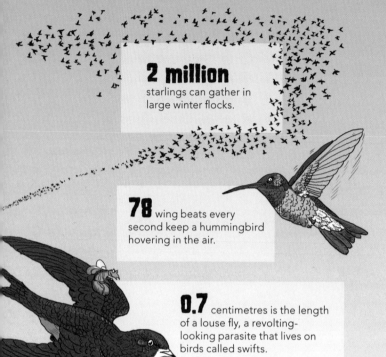

2 million starlings can gather in large winter flocks.

3.5 metres is the biggest wingspan recorded for a wandering albatross – that's as long as 2 average-height men lying end to end.

78 wing beats every second keep a hummingbird hovering in the air.

389 kilometres per hour is the top speed reached by a flying peregrine falcon when it attacks its prey. That's faster than a high speed train.

0.7 centimetres is the length of a louse fly, a revolting-looking parasite that lives on birds called swifts.

15 feathers per square centimetre make emperor penguins more feathery than any other birds.

2,000 tiny feathers are used by long-tailed tits to line their nests. The birds collect these feathers 1 at a time.

6 years is the length of time that a young wandering albatross roams the sea before coming back to land.

36 kilometres per hour is the top speed that the world's fastest-swimming bird – the gentoo penguin – can reach.

9 days is the length of time that birds called bar-tailed godwits can fly for without stopping. These water birds make an epic migration journey from New Zealand to China.

1 in **50,000** penguins is brown and white rather than black and white.

24 billion chickens currently live on planet Earth.

150 words were used by Alex, a famous talking African grey parrot. His last words to his trainer were: 'You be good. See you tomorrow. I love you.'

14 centimetres is the length of a sword-billed hummingbird's beak – but its body is just 10 centimetres long. It has to sit with its beak tilted up, so it doesn't overbalance and fall off its perch.

70 kilometres an hour is the running speed of an ostrich in a hurry.

24 hours after it hatches, a baby mallee fowl is capable of flying.

1,227 species of birds are endangered, out of a total of about 10,000 species.

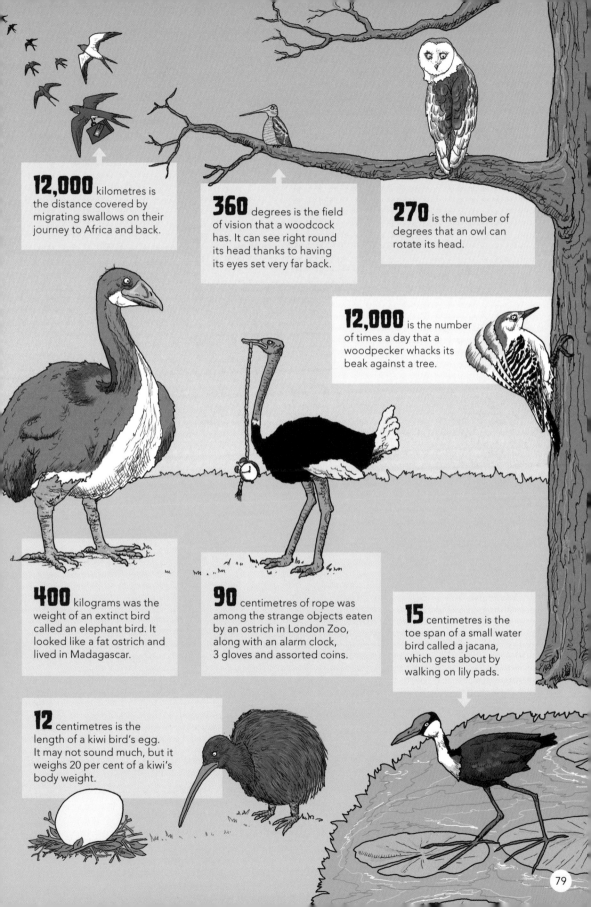

12,000 kilometres is the distance covered by migrating swallows on their journey to Africa and back.

360 degrees is the field of vision that a woodcock has. It can see right round its head thanks to having its eyes set very far back.

270 is the number of degrees that an owl can rotate its head.

12,000 is the number of times a day that a woodpecker whacks its beak against a tree.

400 kilograms was the weight of an extinct bird called an elephant bird. It looked like a fat ostrich and lived in Madagascar.

90 centimetres of rope was among the strange objects eaten by an ostrich in London Zoo, along with an alarm clock, 3 gloves and assorted coins.

15 centimetres is the toe span of a small water bird called a jacana, which gets about by walking on lily pads.

12 centimetres is the length of a kiwi bird's egg. It may not sound much, but it weighs 20 per cent of a kiwi's body weight.

Spooky!

7201 Archer Avenue is where a mysterious female hitchhiker suddenly vanished. This is the address of Chicago's Resurrection Cemetery and the strange passenger is known as Resurrection Mary, one of America's most famous ghosts.

5 buildings are said to be haunted by the ghost of Anne Boleyn, who was beheaded by her husband, King Henry VIII. These are her birthplace (Blickling Hall), her childhood home (Hever Castle), her adult homes (Hampton Court Palace and Windsor Castle) and her place of execution (The Tower of London).

40,000 human skeletons decorate the Church of Bones in Sedlec in the Czech Republic. There is even a large chandelier made out of bones.

180 people were hanged at The Skirrid Inn, in Wales, during its 900 year history. The beam the prisoners were hanged from is still there to this day and guests at the inn report feeling a ghostly noose tightening around their necks.

3,300 years is how long the lonely ghost of a pharaoh called Akhenaten has been wandering the barren Egyptian desert after he was cursed by Egyptian priests.

3 men lived in a lighthouse on the Flannan Isles off the coast of Scotland. When a boat arrived one day in 1900, it found the lighthouse empty. Locals reported seeing a ghostly Viking longship sailing away.

825 kilograms was the weight of a giant Halloween pumpkin carved by an artist called Ray Villafane. The finished work of art featured terrifying zombies crawling out of the pumpkin.

249 is the number of the law in Haiti that makes it a crime to turn a living person into a zombie.

50 years to the day after it sank on February 13th, 1748, a ship called the *Lady Luvibund* was seen sailing off the English coast.

10 women accused of being witches were executed at Lancaster Castle in 1612. 400 years later, the witches are said to still haunt a nearby village called Newchurch, England.

6 million people lie buried in the catacombs of Paris – a maze of tunnels and chambers that run underneath the city. The catacombs have been the place of countless ghostly sightings.

26 witnesses watched in horror as a ghostly army marched over a mountainside at Souter Fell in Scotland in 1745. This army of spooks has visited several times since. It is so large that it can take 2 hours for all the soldiers to march past.

200 small fires mysteriously broke out at a haunted farm in Illinois, USA. Witnesses put them out with buckets of water as soon as they started, but eventually the farm was burned to the ground.

6 degrees Celsius is the approximate drop in temperature when a ghostly presence is reported to be near.

50 cases of Transylvanian soil accompanied Count Dracula on his trip to England in Bram Stoker's famous novel, *Dracula*.

4 ghosts visit Ebenezer Scrooge in Charles Dickens' famous story, *A Christmas Carol*. These are the ghost of his business partner, Jacob Marley, followed by the ghosts of Christmas Past, Christmas Present and Christmas Yet to Come.

10 people had vanished when an abandoned Canadian ship called the *Mary Celeste*, was found floating on the ocean in the Bay of Gibraltar, in 1872. To this day, the mystery has never been solved.

160 kilometres per hour was the speed of a car trying to outrun the Mothman – a strange, winged, man-size creature that reportedly appeared in West Virginia, USA in 1966.

85 was the number given to a vicious gangster called Al Capone when he was sent to a top security prison called Alcatraz, in the USA. While there, he passed the time by learning to play the banjo. The prison no longer has inmates, but it's open to visitors, who have heard the sound of a ghostly banjo playing.

3 mentions of the name Bloody Mary while looking in a mirror with the lights off is said to summon this vengeful ghost.

2.4 metres was the height of Dr Frankenstein' monster in Mary Shelley's famous novel, *Frankenstein*.

376 kilograms is the supposed weight a spooky crying baby spirit grows to when picked up by anyone trying to comfort it. This Japanese spirit, known as a Konaki-jiji crushes the unfortunate, helpful person to death.

8,848 metres high, Mount Everest is said to be haunted by the ghost of Andrew Irvine who died climbing the mountain and whose spirit now helps climbers to the summit.

South America

12 countries are in South America – Argentina, Chile, Peru, Paraguay, Brazil, Ecuador, Uruguay, Venezuela, Colombia, Bolivia, Guyana and Suriname.

7,640 kilometres is the length of the continent from Colombia in the north to the tip of Chile in the south.

6,960 metres above sea level, the Aconcagua Mountain in Argentina is South America's highest mountain. It lies in the Andes mountain range.

30 metres is the height of a statue of Jesus that stands over the Brazilian city of Rio de Janeiro. It is called Christ the Redeemer, and has become one of the world's most recognizable landmarks. Its outstretched arms have a width of 28 metres.

1.35 billion kilograms of coffee are produced by Brazil in a single year.

3 million years ago, South America was joined to North America by an area of land that is now in Panama. The continents have moved over time, so that South America is now connected to Central America.

6,436 kilometres is the length of the mighty Amazon, South America's longest river.

7,240 kilometres is the distance from one end of the Andes mountain range to the other.

8.5 million square kilometres make Brazil South America's largest country.

2 South American countries are landlocked, which means they have no coastline. These are Bolivia and Paraguay.

7 million llamas and alpacas live in South America.

I DON'T THINK IT'S A HAMSTER ...

66 kilograms is the weight the world's largest rodent, the South American capybara, can reach. That's heavier than some adult humans.

984 metres is the height of Venezuela's Angel Falls – the highest waterfall in the world.

9 of South America's 12 countries have Spanish as their official language. The exceptions are Brazil (Portuguese), Suriname (Dutch) and Guyana (English).

91 per cent of Suriname is covered by rainforest.

99 per cent of the world's potatoes come from a species that was originally grown in Chile thousands of years ago.

90 degrees Celsius is the temperature at which water boils in Quito, the capital of Ecuador. The city's height above sea level causes water to boil 10 degrees lower than its normal 100 degree boiling point.

1 millimetre of rain per year is all that falls in the Atacama desert in Chile. In some areas of the desert, not a drop of rain has fallen since records began.

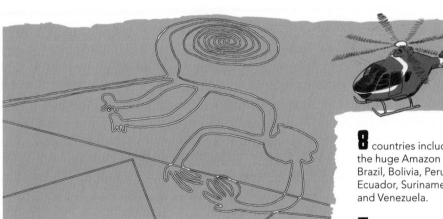

110 metres is the length of a huge drawing of a monkey, scratched into a Peruvian plain between 1,500 and 2,500 years ago. The monkey and many other enormous artworks can still be seen today. They are known as the Nazca Lines.

8 countries include parts of the huge Amazon rainforest: Brazil, Bolivia, Peru, Colombia, Ecuador, Suriname, Guyana and Venezuela.

3 species of vampire bat are native to South (and Central) America. These are the common vampire bat, the hairy-legged vampire bat and the white-winged vampire bat.

17,814,000 square kilometres is the area of the continent of South America.

209,000 cubic meters of water are poured into the Atlantic Ocean by the Amazon River every single second.

47.3 per cent of South America's land is covered by Brazil. It has borders with every South American country except Ecuador and Chile.

Circus Feats

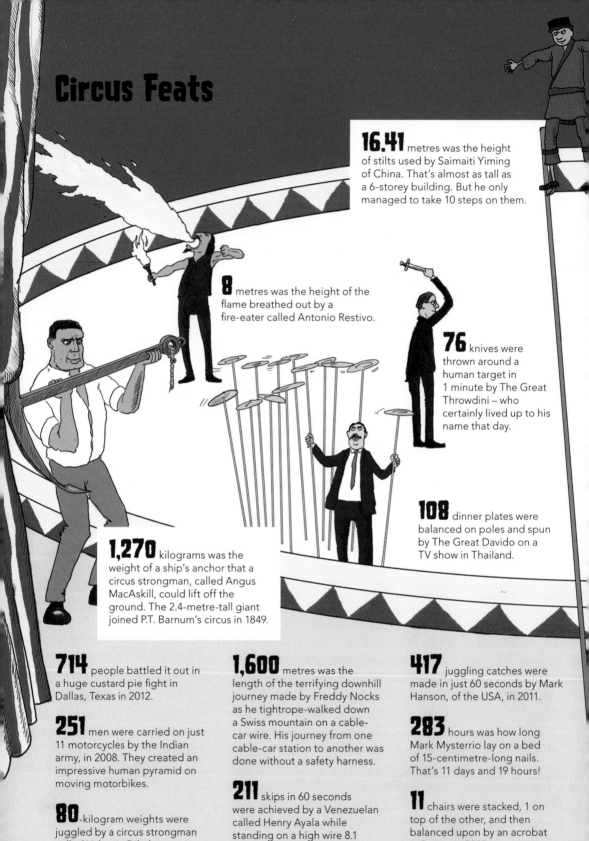

16.41 metres was the height of stilts used by Saimaiti Yiming of China. That's almost as tall as a 6-storey building. But he only managed to take 10 steps on them.

8 metres was the height of the flame breathed out by a fire-eater called Antonio Restivo.

76 knives were thrown around a human target in 1 minute by The Great Throwdini – who certainly lived up to his name that day.

108 dinner plates were balanced on poles and spun by The Great Davido on a TV show in Thailand.

1,270 kilograms was the weight of a ship's anchor that a circus strongman, called Angus MacAskill, could lift off the ground. The 2.4-metre-tall giant joined P.T. Barnum's circus in 1849.

714 people battled it out in a huge custard pie fight in Dallas, Texas in 2012.

251 men were carried on just 11 motorcycles by the Indian army, in 2008. They created an impressive human pyramid on moving motorbikes.

80-kilogram weights were juggled by a circus strongman called Valentin Dikul.

1,600 metres was the length of the terrifying downhill journey made by Freddy Nocks as he tightrope-walked down a Swiss mountain on a cable-car wire. His journey from one cable-car station to another was done without a safety harness.

211 skips in 60 seconds were achieved by a Venezuelan called Henry Ayala while standing on a high wire 8.1 metres above ground.

417 juggling catches were made in just 60 seconds by Mark Hanson, of the USA, in 2011.

283 hours was how long Mark Mysterrio lay on a bed of 15-centimetre-long nails. That's 11 days and 19 hours!

11 chairs were stacked, 1 on top of the other, and then balanced upon by an acrobat in Bejing in 2007.

2.9 metres is the height that Dan Mahoney can leap on a pogo stick.

5,000 shots out of a cannon make David Smith a very experienced human cannonball. He can fly as far as 59 metres.

747 balloon sculptures were completed in 1 hour by a comedian and balloon artist called John Cassidy. That's more than 12 per minute!

305 hula hoops were spun round Jin Linlin's body at the same time.

58 was the size of the enormous clown shoes worn by Coco the Clown.

7 flaming torches were juggled by Anthony Gasso of the USA in 1989.

10,000 spectators could be seated at P.T. Barnum's 19th-century circus, called the Greatest Show on Earth.

175 stitches were needed by a fearless circus tiger tamer called Mabel Stark, when one of her tigers attacked her in 1915.

1,300 clowns have graduated from Ringling Brothers Clown College.

10,000 clowns live in Mexico.

2,194 metres above ground and hanging upside down from a rope, a magician called Scott Hammell managed to escape from a straitjacket.

2,945 kilometres was the distance of the route taken by Sylvian Dornon in 1891, when he walked on stilts from Paris to Moscow.

3-year-old Cranston Chipperfield was the Circus Royale's ringmaster in 2005. He became the eighth generation of the Chipperfield family to become a ringmaster.

Going Underground

240 pounds was the amount a Scotsman called David Booth spent buying a metal detector. The very first time he used it outdoors he discovered 4 gold necklaces that were 2,000 years old. Booth received £462,000 for his finds.

2 thumbs are on each of a mole's front paws. The 2 pairs of thumbs help the mole dig underground more efficiently.

360 glass items, watches and other jewellery were all found in a secret underground room in Christchurch, New Zealand, when an office block was demolished.

1,200 shops can be found below ground in 28 kilometres of shopping arcades in Toronto. It's the largest underground shopping centre in the world.

36,852 books were left on London Underground trains in a single year. Among the oddest things lost on the trains were a lawnmower, a human skull and a park bench.

1.1 billion passengers are carried in the London Underground's 4,134 passenger trains each year.

9,550-year-old roots that belong to a spruce tree are still growing in the soil in Sweden.

800 metres beneath the mountains in the Alps, you can find the Gotthard rail tunnel. It is 57 kilometres long.

3.9 kilometres below the ground is the world's deepest mine – the TauTona gold mine in South Africa.

2.5 football pitches is the size of a huge underground lake. It is found 60 metres below ground in Namibia, and is called Dragon's Breath.

1,695 people live in an Australian mining town called Coober Pedy. Many of them live in underground homes to keep away from the scorching heat above ground.

90 is the number of different entrances a meerkat colony's burrow may have.

4,000 people, including the government, were expected to live in a large underground city in the UK, called Burlington, if there was a nuclear attack. The top-secret city featured offices, a radio studio, laundries and 2 large kitchens.

40 per cent of all the gold ever mined has come from underground mines in the Witwatersrand Basin, a region of South Africa.

120 litres of grain and seeds may be stored by a tiny kangaroo rat in its underground burrow.

8.5 centimetres long and weighing 35 grams, the rhinoceros cockroach is the biggest cockroach in the world. It burrows around 1 metre down into soil to make a home.

21 ancient Roman coins were found buried in a field in England by an amateur treasure hunter called Dave Crisp in 2010. Eventually, a staggering 52,503 coins were found there.

20,000 different species of bacteria can sometimes be found in 1 gram of soil.

1.8 kilometres is the length of the world's shortest underground metro system, in Haifa, Israel. It has just 6 stations.

14 states of America were passed through on a secret network of routes to help slaves escape to freedom in Canada. It was called the Underground Railroad, but it was in fact neither underground, nor a railroad! It was given this name because its activities had to be kept secret and people helping the slaves often used railway terms as a sort of code.

40 centimetres is the length of a blind cave eel. It has no eyes and lives in water flowing in underground caves in Australia.

Knights and Castles

300 castles still stand in England.

14 years was the length of a knight's training in the Middle Ages – 7 years as a servant called a page, followed by another 7 years as a trainee knight, called a squire.

7 gates have to be passed to reach the castle inside Mehrangarh Fort in India.

50 kilograms was how much a medieval knight's armour could weigh. That's like carrying around a baby hippo.

6,000 people a day visit Neuschwanstein Castle in Germany. This beautiful, fairy-tale castle inspired Walt Disney's Magic Kingdom.

1 castle is owned by the British Queen. This is Balmoral Castle in Scotland. Although she lives in Windsor Castle for much of the year, she does not own this building (nor does she own Buckingham Palace).

83 buildings are inside Himeji Castle, a wooden castle in Japan.

950 years is how long the British royal family have lived in Windsor Castle. This makes it the oldest castle to have been lived in without a break.

1,051 metres is the length of Germany's Burghausen Castle. It's the longest castle in the world.

1,481 steps have to be climbed to reach Poenari Castle in Romania.

95 kilometres per hour was the speed at which 2 jousting knights clashed.

4 metres was the length of a typical lance used by knights in jousting tournaments.

3,700 metres above sea level lies Tibet's Potala Palace, high up in the Himalayan mountains. This castle has over 1,000 rooms.

400 stonemasons were employed to build one of King Edward I of England's castles.

40 days of military service each year was the amount of time a medieval knight had to promise to his lord or king.

14,248 pounds was the cost of building the mighty Conwy Castle, in Wales, which is now a World Heritage Site.

6 metres is the thickness of some castle walls.

228 metres was the distance from which an arrow fired from a medieval longbow could pierce a knight's armour.

84 different staircases can be climbed in a magnificent French castle called Château de Chambord.

7 knightly virtues make up the knight's code of chivalry (good behaviour). These are: courage, justice, mercy, generosity, faith, nobility and hope.

122 metres was the depth of a well that provided water for the people who lived in Beeston Castle in England.

9 metres could be the depth of water-filled defensive ditches called moats that surrounded castles.

3 different-coloured shields displaying tears were hung at a famous tournament called the Fountain of Tears in medieval France. Challengers who chose the white shield would fight with axes, choosing the violet shield meant fighting with swords, and picking the black shield led to a battle with lances.

300 lances had to be broken in jousts before a knight called Suero de Quiñones would end his tournament. Contests like this were called Pas d'Armes and could last for months.

5,000 soldiers could be housed in a huge castle in Syria called the Krak des Chevaliers. Its store rooms were so big they could hold 5 years' worth of supplies.

52 towers, 3 kilometres of walls and 1 huge castle protect a fortified French town called Carcassonne.

6 tonnes is the weight of Mons Meg, a 15th century cannon that protects Edinburgh Castle.

6 miles of labyrinths lie under Buda Castle in Hungary. The labyrinth was once a prison, whose most famous resident was a murderous ruler known as Vlad the Impaler.

Perfect Primates

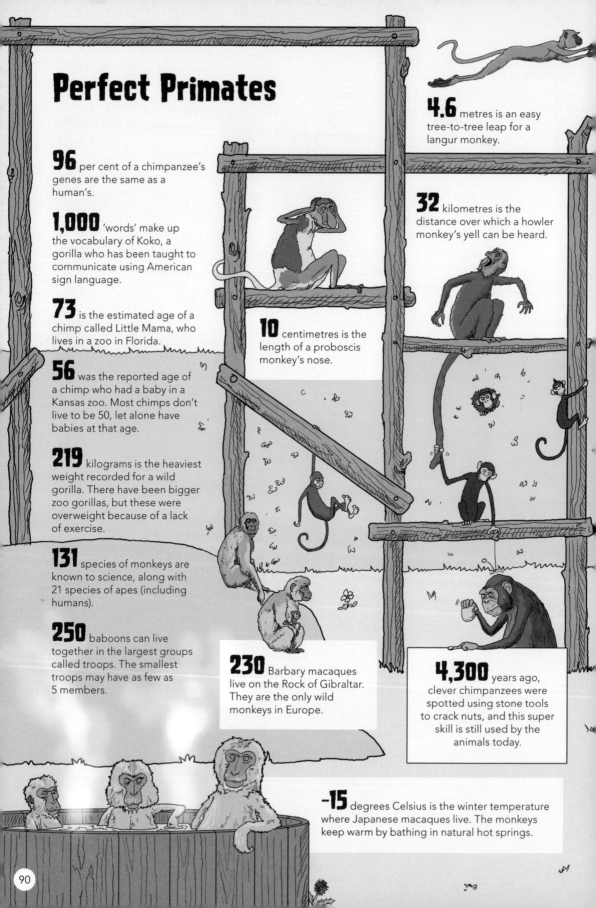

4.6 metres is an easy tree-to-tree leap for a langur monkey.

96 per cent of a chimpanzee's genes are the same as a human's.

1,000 'words' make up the vocabulary of Koko, a gorilla who has been taught to communicate using American sign language.

73 is the estimated age of a chimp called Little Mama, who lives in a zoo in Florida.

56 was the reported age of a chimp who had a baby in a Kansas zoo. Most chimps don't live to be 50, let alone have babies at that age.

219 kilograms is the heaviest weight recorded for a wild gorilla. There have been bigger zoo gorillas, but these were overweight because of a lack of exercise.

131 species of monkeys are known to science, along with 21 species of apes (including humans).

250 baboons can live together in the largest groups called troops. The smallest troops may have as few as 5 members.

10 centimetres is the length of a proboscis monkey's nose.

32 kilometres is the distance over which a howler monkey's yell can be heard.

230 Barbary macaques live on the Rock of Gibraltar. They are the only wild monkeys in Europe.

4,300 years ago, clever chimpanzees were spotted using stone tools to crack nuts, and this super skill is still used by the animals today.

-15 degrees Celsius is the winter temperature where Japanese macaques live. The monkeys keep warm by bathing in natural hot springs.

3 different alarm calls are used by vervet monkeys to warn of danger. One means snake, one means eagle and the last means leopard.

22 Hainan gibbons are all that's estimated to be left in the wild, making this animal an endangered species.

500 pounds is the amount of money called a monkey in old English slang. The nickname comes from soldiers who served in India, where a 500-rupee bank note used to have a picture of a monkey on it.

116 days is the length of time a desert troop of baboons survived without water when the rains were late.

600 milligrams of vitamin C is consumed each day by an average 7-kilogram monkey. That's 10 times the amount recommended for a 70-kilogram human.

15 hours of sleep a day keeps a gorilla feeling chirpy for the few hours it's awake.

2.74 metres was the height of the largest ape ever to have existed, an extinct human-like creature called Gigantopithecus. That's about half the height of a giraffe.

1.5 metres is the arm-span of a large siamang gibbon. That's 0.5 metres more than its body length.

16 minutes was the length of the space flight experienced by 2 monkeys in 1959. Miss Able the rhesus monkey and Miss Baker the squirrel monkey were the first animals ever to survive space travel.

5 centimetres is the length of a big male baboon's canine teeth.

10 different colours are found on a male mandrill.

54 kilograms is the weight of a hugely heavy male mandrill. Females are half the size of males.

Survival Stories

9 bullets hit Wenseslao Moguel when he faced a firing squad during the Mexican Revolution. Astonishingly, he survived.

9.6 kilometres of swimming through shark-infested seas led Sophie Tucker, a family's pet dog who had fallen from a yacht, to a small island off the Australian coast. She was reunited with her owners after living wild on the island for 4 months.

7 weeks is how long 2 Frenchmen survived on a diet of spiders, frogs, centipedes and turtles after getting lost in the jungle of French Guyana.

9 days after being trapped under rubble in a Japanese earthquake, 16-year-old Jin Abe and his 80-year-old grandmother were finally rescued alive.

7 days is how long a camel can easily survive without water.

52 months was the length of time a man named Alexander Selkirk spent marooned on an uninhabited island before being rescued. His story inspired a novel called *Robinson Crusoe*.

6 terrifying days was the length of time a 76-year-old Cypriot woman spent trapped in a lift. All she had to eat in that time were a few tomatoes.

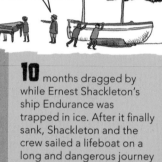

I TOLD YOU WE'RE NOT TAKING IT!

10 months dragged by while Ernest Shackleton's ship Endurance was trapped in ice. After it finally sank, Shackleton and the crew sailed a lifeboat on a long and dangerous journey to a whaling station on the island of South Georgia.

2 years were spent teaching an African grey parrot to repeat its name and address. One day the parrot flew off and got lost. It was captured and taken to a vet. Amazingly, it told the vet where it lived and was safely returned home to its owners.

33 men were trapped deep underground in Chile's San José Mine for 69 days before all were safely rescued in 2010.

GREAT NEWS! THE VACCINE HAS ARRIVED.

1,085 kilometres was the distance a dog team pulled a sled across the frozen Alaskan landscape to deliver a vaccine to the town of Nome. The town was struck by a disease called diphtheria in 1925.

8 wild cats huddled around a lost one-year-old boy to keep him warm during the freezing nights he spent on the streets of an Argentinian city.

15-metre-high waves rolled Tami Oldham Ashcraft's boat over and upright again during a hurricane. She was knocked out and awoke a day later to find the boat's engine and equipment destroyed and her crewmate missing. She finally reached land 42 days later.

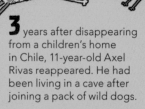

3 years after disappearing from a children's home in Chile, 11-year-old Axel Rivas reappeared. He had been living in a cave after joining a pack of wild dogs.

194 soldiers' lives were saved thanks to the bravery of a First-World-War messenger pigeon called Cher Ami. Although shot in the leg and breast, he completed his mission, delivering a message that helped rescue a lost battalion. He was awarded a medal for his bravery.

11 days was the amount of time that a 62-year-old called Teresa Bordais spent stuck at the bottom of a deep ravine in Spain. She survived on leaves and rainwater until her rescue.

4 months is how long 14-year-old D'Zhana Simmons from the USA survived without a heart. A blood-pumping machine kept her alive until she finally had a heart transplant.

299 kilometres off course, Italian runner Mauro Prosperi was finally found by desert nomads after losing his way during the 1994 'Marathon des Sables', a 233-kilometre running race across the Sahara Desert. He had been missing for 9 days and had lost 18 kilograms in weight.

124 kilometres from her home, a dog called Moon became separated from her owner. She arrived home in Nevada, USA, 8 days later, after having walked all the way. The journey would have taken her across a desert and 2 mountain ranges.

155 lives were saved by quick-thinking pilot Captain Sullenberger, who made an emergency landing in New York's Hudson River after the plane he was flying lost power.

2 months after being trapped by snow in his car in a remote part of Sweden, Peter Skyllberg was found alive.

470 metres under the sea, a minisub called *Pisces III* lay damaged on the ocean floor. After the deepest ever underwater rescue, its 2 crew members were saved just before their air supplies ran out.

The Rainforest

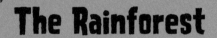

5.4 million square kilometres is the area of the Amazon rainforest.

6 per cent of the world's surface is currently covered by rainforest. In the 1950s, however, this figure was 14 per cent.

200,000 native Indian people live in the Amazon rainforest.

137 rainforest plant and animal species are being wiped out every single day, scientists estimate.

3,700 square kilometres is the size of the Gondwana rainforest in Australia, the largest area of subtropical rainforest in the world.

4 distinct layers (from ground to sky) make up a rainforest – the forest floor, the understorey, the canopy and the emergent layer.

52,000 square kilometres of Amazon rainforest are being destroyed every year.

43 different species of ants can live in just one Peruvian rainforest tree.

1,500 different species of flowering plants grow in 0.01 square kilometres of rainforest.

5 species of great apes exist in the world. Examples of all of these live in rainforest areas.

78 teeth are packed into a spectacled caiman's mouth. This is a kind of crocodile that lives in the Amazon.

130 million years old is the age of some ancient rainforest in Borneo.

80 metres is the height of the tallest rainforest trees.

200 million cows live in Brazil, many on ranches that were created by clearing areas of rainforest.

1 per cent of rainforest plant species have so far been properly studied by scientists.

254 centimetres of rain fall in a rainforest each year.

80 per cent of the foods we eat originally came from rainforests. These include bananas, potatoes, avocados, tomatoes, black pepper, coffee and sugar.

70,000 people visit the Monteverde Cloud Forest reserve in Costa Rica each year, to enjoy its amazing rainforest wildlife.

3,300 metres above sea level is the upper limit of most mountain rainforests.

20 per cent of all the oxygen in our atmosphere is made by the trees and other plants in the Amazon rainforest.

10 minutes is the time it takes for rain to make its way from the top of the rainforest canopy to the ground.

48 different species of birds flock together to search for food in the Sinharaja forest in Sri Lanka.

1,000 years is the age of some of the spruce and cedar trees in certain rainforests.

27 degrees Celsius is the average temperature inside a tropical rainforest, at any time of year.

7.7 millimetres is the size of a tiny frog called Paedophryne amauensis, which lives in the rainforests of Papua New Guinea.

5 of the world's continents have tropical rainforests – Africa, Asia, Australasia and North and South America.

3,000 different kinds of fruit can be found in the world's rainforests. In the western world, we only eat about 200 of these.

1 rainforest reserve, found in Peru, contains more species of bird than can be found in the entire United States of America.

25 per cent of the medicines we use contain ingredients from rainforest plants or animals.

4.6 metres a minute is the fastest a super-slow sloth can move through the rainforest trees.

2 per cent of sunlight reaches the rainforest floor. Plants that grow in this near-darkness can't survive in brighter light.

Africa

54 countries make up the continent of Africa – from Tunisia in the north to South Africa in the south.

5,895 metres above sea level, Mount Kilimanjaro in Tanzania is Africa's tallest mountain.

7 tonnes at its heaviest, an African elephant is the largest land animal in the world.

4 seas surround Africa – the Mediterranean in the north, the Atlantic in the west, the Indian Ocean in the east and the Red Sea in the north-east.

80 species of lemur live on the island of Madagascar, the only place in the world they can be found in the wild.

6,650 kilometres long, the Nile is the longest river in the world.

6 African countries are on the Equator – Gabon, Congo, Democratic Republic of Congo, Uganda, Kenya and Somalia.

11 centuries is how long the world's oldest university in Fez, Morocco, has been educating students.

4,500 rock paintings have been found at Tsodilo in Botswana. This small part of the Kalahari Desert has been given the nickname of the Louvre of the Desert, after a famous art gallery in Paris, France called the Louvre.

HERE COMES LUNCH!

1.3 million wildebeest, **300,000** gazelle and **200,000** zebra live on an East African plain called the Serengeti.

8 per cent of the world's ocean-going ships pass through Egypt's Suez Canal, a 163-kilometre-long waterway which links the Mediterranean to the Red Sea. It can save ships thousands of miles in their journey between east and west.

9.1 million square kilometres make the Sahara the largest sand desert on Earth.

1,000–2,000 is the estimated number of languages spoken in Africa. It is difficult to be exact as some languages have no written system and some are spoken by very small numbers of people.

100 metres long and **40** metres wide, the Grand Mosque in Djenne, Mali, is the largest mud building in the world.

15 million Africans were sent to America to become slaves between the 15th and 19th centuries.

230 metres is the depth the Congo River can reach. That's deep enough to submerge the Statue of Liberty and the clock tower in London known as Big Ben if they were stacked on top of each other.

223 pyramids were built in Sudan over 2,000 years ago, so it is not just Egypt that has these famous structures.

660 kilometres is the length from shore to shore of Lake Tanganyika.

48 per cent of the world's diamonds come from Africa.

1 million flamingos flock to Lake Natron in Tanzania each year to breed on the lake's islands.

1 of the original **7** Wonders of the ancient World still exists – the Great Pyramid of Giza in Egypt.

305 metres is the height of some spectacular sand dunes that can be found in the Namib Desert.

10 per cent of the world's bird, fish and plant species are found in South Africa.

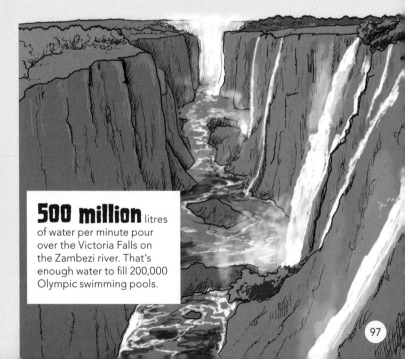

500 million litres of water per minute pour over the Victoria Falls on the Zambezi river. That's enough water to fill 200,000 Olympic swimming pools.

The Sun

149.6 million kilometres is the distance that heat and light travel from the Sun to the Earth.

1.4 million kilometres is the width of the Sun.

99.8 per cent of all the mass in the Solar System is contained in the Sun.

Mercury   Venus   Earth   Mars

15 minutes is the amount of time it's recommended for you to expose your face, neck and arms to sunlight every day, in order for your body to make enough vitamin D to keep you healthy.

5 billion years is the estimated life that the Sun has left. After this it will expand and become a Red Giant, which is the name for a dying star.

98 per cent of harmful rays from the Sun are blocked by the average factor 50 sunscreen.

4.5 million tonnes of the material of the Sun gets blown off into space every single second by the solar winds.

28 is the number of times stronger the gravity is on the Sun than on Earth.

4.6 billion years is the length of time that the Sun is thought to have been shining.

8 planets orbit the Sun, not counting Pluto, which is now classified as a dwarf planet.

8.19 minutes is the amount of time it takes for light to travel from the Sun to the Earth.

5.9 billion kilometres is the distance between the Sun and the dwarf planet, Pluto. The Sun's gravitational pull is so strong, that Pluto is still affected by it from so far away.

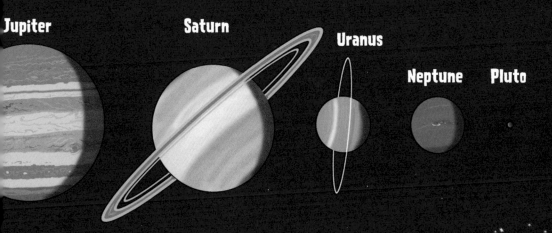

Jupiter **Saturn** **Uranus** **Neptune** **Pluto**

400,000 times is how much brighter the Sun is than the Moon.

71 per cent of the Sun is made up of a gas called hydrogen.

400 kilometres per second is the speed of charged particles that come out of the Sun. These are known as solar winds.

80,000 kilometres is the width that some sunspots can reach. Sunspots are darker patches on the surface of the Sun that are much cooler than their surrounding areas.

1.3 million planet Earths could fit inside the Sun if it was hollow.

15.5 million degrees Celsius is the temperature of the Sun's core.

100 billion tonnes is the amount of dynamite you would have to explode every second in order to match the energy that the Sun produces.

225 million years is the time it takes for the Sun to complete an orbit of the Milky Way Galaxy.

40 per cent is how much brighter the Sun shines today, compared with its brightness when planet Earth was formed. Scientists calculate that the Sun becomes 10 per cent brighter every billion years.

7.5 minutes is the longest time that a total solar eclipse (when the Moon passes between the Sun and the Earth and blocks out the Sun) can last for, because of the speed at which the Sun is travelling.

800,000 kilometres per hour is the speed that the Sun travels as it orbits the centre of the Milky Way Galaxy.

Hair and Fur

100 roubles a year was the tax any Russian with a beard had to pay Peter the Great, the ruler of Russia in the 17th Century. They were then given a beard licence, which read: The beard is a useless burden.

115 different famous heads have contributed hair to a man called John Reznikoff's collection. It includes locks from Abraham Lincoln, Marilyn Monroe, Albert Einstein, Napoleon and Charles Dickens.

100 hairs per day fall out of an average person's head.

50 eggs can be laid each day by a single flea in a dog's or cat's fur.

12.7 centimetres was the diameter of a fur ball found in the stomach of a cat called Gemma. Fur balls are caused by cats licking themselves clean and accidentally swallowing some of the fur. They don't usually get this large though.

6 years without stopping is how long a strand of hair grows for, before it stops for a few months and then falls out.

150,000 hairs are on an average person's head.

5 hairy eyes peer out from a bee's face. Yes, that's right – they actually have hair on their eyes!

2 sets of eyelashes grow on each of a camel's eyes. They help to keep out the desert sand.

3 times – this is how much deeper the root of a cat's whisker is set into the skin than a normal hair. This makes whiskers really sensitive, so they can help cats pick up useful information.

25 tiny bugs called eyelash mites may live on 1 single eyelash.

13.5 centimetres was the record-breaking length of an upper-arm hair belonging to a teenager called Robert Starrett.

27.9 centimetres was the length of the longest hair in V. Wheeler's beard. What makes this particularly impressive is that the V stands for Vivian and the beard belonged to a woman!

90 centimetres is the length that a musk ox's hair can grow to. That's the longest hair of any wild animal.

200 tiny hairs make up each of your eyelashes.

115,120 dollars were paid by a fan for hair clippings belonging to the king of rock 'n' roll, Elvis Presley.

132,000–155,000 hairs per square centimetre give sea otters the thickest fur of any mammal.

5 different fur colours mean the American black bear is not always black. It can be black, brown, blonde, cinnamon or white.

0.03 millimetres is the width of a typical strand of hair.

10,000 years old is the age of some woolly mammoth hair discovered preserved in the frozen ground of Siberia.

1 centimetre per month is the speed hair grows. This means it would take hair 833 years to complete a 100-metre race.

4 days walking around with porcupine hair on your head was regarded as a way to cure baldness by the ancient Egyptians.

2 layers of fur keep polar bears warm and dry. A short layer keeps the bear warm, while an outer, longer layer keeps water away from the short fur.

8 pairs of scissors were held in one hand by a hairdresser called Bruce Choy in the USA, and used to style a customer's hair.

5.6 metres was the length of Xie Qiuping's hair when it was measured. She had not cut it for 40 years.

114 centimetres is the height from head to tip of Kazuhiro Watanabe's mohican haircut. It's a spectacular sight.

3,744 hairstyles were included in the first hair magazine published in Paris in 1772. Some of them were so elaborate, the hairdresser would have needed a stepladder to complete them.

Diseases

33 months is how long a colony of bacteria survived on the Moon. A sneeze into a video camera accidentally left the bacteria there. When the camera was recovered nearly 3 years later, the bacteria were still alive.

25 million Europeans died during an outbreak of Bubonic plague between 1347 and 1352. That's 1 in every 3 people. The plague is better known by its nickname of The Black Death.

8 million germs can be created in a single day from just 1 original germ. This is because some bacteria can divide every 20 minutes.

2,000 sufferers of the King's Evil were touched by Louis XV of France in the 18th century. The King's Evil was a skin disease known as scrofula and it was believed a touch from the king could cure it.

25 million people in the world are at risk of contracting malaria, which is a disease spread by mosquitoes.

90 per cent of people are naturally immune to leprosy.

7 of every **10** people have gum disease, making it the world's most common disease.

21 days is the amount of time it can take to get spots after being exposed to chicken pox.

30 people have been known to be allergic to water, making life very difficult indeed for the sufferers.

75 per cent of diseases that have recently appeared in humans are zoonotic. This means they came from animals.

60 recorded cases of Foreign Accent Syndrome have been recorded. Those suffering from it inexplicably begin to talk with a foreign accent.

0.0005 millimetres is the size of the smallest bacteria ever found. Bacteria are the smallest living things in the world.

2 days is the average time it takes a person to become ill after they have been exposed to the flu virus.

400 people caught a bizarre dancing disease in 16th-century France. Sufferers would dance uncontrollably for days until they dropped with exhaustion.

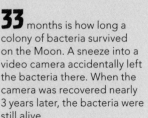

91 per cent was the fall in measles infections in Africa between 2000 and 2006, thanks to a vaccination campaign.

7,000 rare diseases are known to exist. A rare disease is one that affects less than 1 in 2,000 people.

10,000 white blood cells may be contained in a single drop of blood. These cells defend the body from diseases.

161 kilometres per hour is the speed at which a sneeze can travel.

3,000 drops of saliva are shot out of the mouth in just one cough.

47,529 flu vaccines were given in just 8 hours during a vaccination campaign in California, USA, in 2012.

5 million bacteria live on every square centimetre of the human body.

200 is the number of colds you are likely to catch in your lifetime.

80 per cent of the crew, led by a famous explorer called Magellan, died from scurvy when they crossed the Pacific in 1520. Scurvy is caused by lack of vitamin C and is easily prevented by eating fruit and vegetables.

42 degrees Celsius is the point at which a feverish person's body starts to shut down. A normal body temperature is 37 degrees.

10 million people were cured of leprosy between 1983 and 1998.

0 people have contracted smallpox in the 21st century. This terrible disease was wiped out in the 20th century, with the world being declared smallpox free in 1979.

100 tourists in Florence, Italy, were studied by doctors and scientists for symptoms of Stendhal Syndrome. This disease causes dizziness, heart flutters, feelings of stress and sometimes fainting, when in the presence of great works of art.

90 per cent of females wash their hands after going to the toilet, but only 67 per cent of males do.

0.5 millimetres is the diameter of bacteria found in sediment off the African coast. This is so big, the bacteria can actually be seen with the naked eye.

The Vikings

9 worlds existed in Viking mythology. Midgard was the world of humans, but there were also worlds populated by gods, giants, elves, dwarves, the dead and demons.

3 countries were the homelands of the Vikings – Norway, Sweden and Denmark.

30,000 metal links made up a single chain mail shirt worn by a Viking warrior for protection in battle.

0 horns were worn on Viking helmets. This well-known decoration was made up by writers and film-makers.

3 goddesses of fate, the Norns, span the threads of life which decided the fate of all living creatures. These goddesses of Norse mythology were called Urd (past), Verdani (present) and Skuld (future).

189 cows was the fine that had to be paid for murdering someone in some Viking lands.

1 bath a week led to the Vikings being seen as obsessed with cleanliness by the Saxons, who only bathed once a year.

19 brothers were killed by their sole surviving brother, Erik, who, not surprisingly, went by the nickname Erik Bloodaxe.

4 Vikings became kings of England – Sweyn Forkbeard, Canute, Harald Harefoot and Hardicanute.

54 headless Vikings were found in a grave in southern England in 2009. Their heads were piled up at the side.

27 years was the length of the reign of a Danish king called Harald Bluetooth (958–985). He was killed in battle against his own son.

12-year-old Vagn Åkesson was allowed to join a group called the Jomsvikings after defeating a warrior in combat. Jomsvikings normally had a minimum joining age of 18.

30 pairs of Viking skis, made from pine, have been found by archeologists. Skates made of animal bones have also been found.

24 letters were used in the Vikings' alphabet, which was known as the Runes.

20 centimetres is the length of a fossilized Viking poo at York's Viking museum. That's the largest ancient poo in any museum collection!

150 centimetres was the length of large, double-handed axes that brought terror to the Vikings' enemies.

120-centimetre-tall shields were used by the Vikings to form a shield wall in battle and stop the enemy getting through.

60 stones were used to form the outline of a stone ship at Gettlinge, in Sweden. These ships surrounded burial sites.

40 to **60** Vikings could sail in 1 Viking longship.

200 ships took a Viking army to the Battle of Stamford Bridge in northern England in 1066. So many Vikings were killed by the Saxons that only 25 ships were needed to take the survivors home.

5 Viking ships were found in a narrow strip of sea called the Roskilde fjord in Denmark in the 1960s. There is now a Viking museum there, where visitors can see the ships.

300 Viking ships formed an invasion force that attacked King Alfred in the kingdom of Wessex in south-west England in 892.

500 years or so before Christopher Columbus set sail to America, the Vikings had already reached the country by sailing right across the Atlantic.

25 ships full of settlers were tricked into sailing to a large, icy land in the north Atlantic. A Viking called Eric the Red named it Greenland to encourage people to move there in 980.

Toys and Games

311 million tiny tyres were made by Lego® for their little vehicles in 2001.

2 Barbie™ dolls are sold somewhere in the world every single second.

350 million Rubik's Cubes® have been sold worldwide. If you stacked all of them on top of each other, they would be 1,937 times taller than Mount Everest.

20 different responses can be given by a fortune-telling toy called a Magic 8 Ball™. Ask the Ball a question, then turn it over and watch as an answer appears through a mysterious blue liquid in a small transparent window.

24 metres of coiled wire make up an original Slinky toy – a spring that can walk down stairs.

15 (again!)

15 is the age of a popular blue videogame character called Sonic the Hedgehog. He never gets any older.

100-yen coins temporarily ran out in Japan in 1978, because people were using so many of them to play a new arcade game called Space Invaders.

16,029 dollars were paid at an auction for a yoyo signed by US President Richard Nixon.

42 holes are in a Connect Four® grid. Players must choose a colour and take turns dropping their counters into the grid, trying to line up 4 in a row.

1,008 polka dot mats were used in a huge game of Twister®, which took place at a high school in the USA for charity.

30,000 games of Scrabble™ are started every hour somewhere in the world.

12 parts make up a lavish doll's house, owned by a 1930s actress called Colleen Moore. The doll's house is known as The Fairy Castle and includes miniature chandeliers hung with real diamonds, paintings painted by Walt Disney himself, and a silver bathtub with little dolphin statues that squirt water.

20 hours can be spent on a single Etch-A-Sketch image by an artist called Jeff Gagliardi. The Etch A Sketch® is a toy with two dials to create simple drawings on a screen. Jeff uses the toy to recreate the works of some of the world's most famous artists, from Leonardo da Vinci, to Pablo Picasso.

1 million Mr Potato Heads™ sold in 1952 – the toy's first year. For the first 12 years of its existence, children had to use real spuds to create their potato pals. In 1964, a plastic potato body was included to stop the risk of the toy going rotten.

125 different careers have been undertaken by the popular doll Barbie™, including a fashion designer, a nurse, a vet and an astronaut.

67 Lego® people exist for every 1 human on the planet.

605 million people around the world know how to play chess.

1.5 billion toys are sold every year by fast food company McDonalds. This makes them one of the biggest toy manufacturers in the world.

6 murder suspects are featured in the original version of a board game called Cluedo®. These are: Colonel Mustard, Professor Plum, Reverend Green, Mrs Peacock, Miss Scarlet and Mrs White.

54 wooden blocks are used in a game of Jenga®. The aim of the game is to remove blocks from a tower one at a time, and place them back on the top to make a taller tower. The loser is the first one to knock it over.

25 tonnes is the weight of an enormous rocking horse in South Australia. Visitors can climb the giant horse and receive a certificate if they reach the top.

1,080 hours was the length of time an epic underwater Monopoly® tournament lasted for. Yes … underwater! The players were teams of scuba divers, and the board was specially made to cope in watery conditions.

2.1 million dollars was paid at an auction for a teddy bear made by a German company, called Steiff. The bear is dressed in clothes made by a famous fashion designer called Louis Vuitton, and it now lives in a teddy bear museum in Korea.

930 model trains take to the tracks every day on the biggest model railway in the world. This fantastic tiny railroad can be found in the Miniatur Wunderland in Hamburg, Germany.

Foodie Facts

15,433 grains of wheat are needed to make 1 kilogram of wholemeal flour.

875,000 chocolate chips would give you enough energy to walk around the world.

100,000 puffed-up grains of rice are in a box of crispy rice cereal. It crackles when milk is added, as the sudden change in temperature causes the thin walls of the puffed up rice to break.

130 milligrams of vitamin C are in a serving of kale (a type of cabbage). That's almost twice the amount found in an orange.

50 to **100** taste receptors are found on each of your tongue's tastebuds. You have tastebuds for sweet, bitter, sour, savoury and salty flavours.

38 degrees Celsius is the temperature of milk when it comes out of a cow.

8 years and **7** months is how long you'd have to scream for to produce enough sound energy to heat up 1 cup of coffee.

340 kilograms was the weight of the first microwave oven. Percy LeBaron Spencer invented it after a chocolate bar melted in his pocket when he walked past a piece of equipment called a radar tube.

11 rodent hairs is the maximum number of rodent hairs allowed in every 50 grams of cinnamon.

8 per cent of the weight of a box of cornflakes is actually made up of corn.

20 per cent of the pineapple in a can is legally allowed to be mouldy.

4,000 different types of tomato exist worldwide.

500 years ago, carrots were purple. The orange carrot we know and love today was cultivated in the 16th century by Dutch growers, from white and yellow mutant carrots.

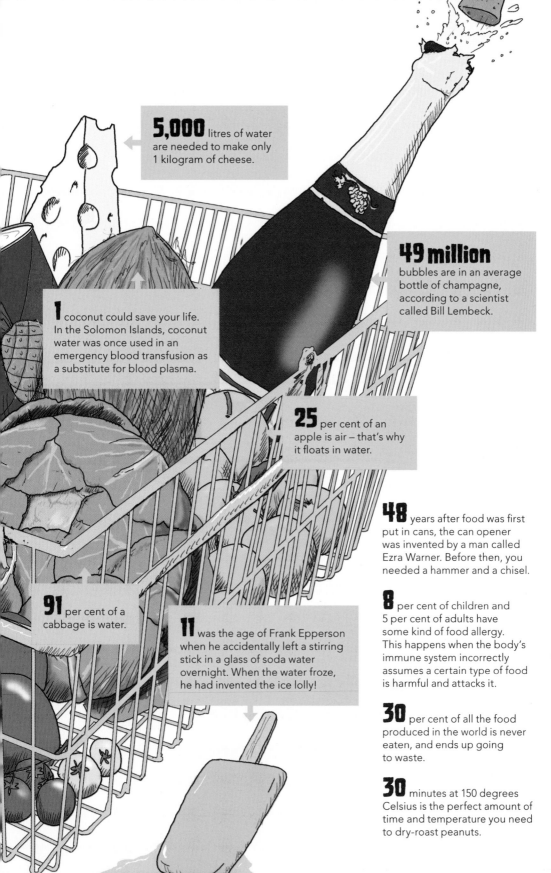

5,000 litres of water are needed to make only 1 kilogram of cheese.

49 million bubbles are in an average bottle of champagne, according to a scientist called Bill Lembeck.

1 coconut could save your life. In the Solomon Islands, coconut water was once used in an emergency blood transfusion as a substitute for blood plasma.

25 per cent of an apple is air – that's why it floats in water.

48 years after food was first put in cans, the can opener was invented by a man called Ezra Warner. Before then, you needed a hammer and a chisel.

91 per cent of a cabbage is water.

11 was the age of Frank Epperson when he accidentally left a stirring stick in a glass of soda water overnight. When the water froze, he had invented the ice lolly!

8 per cent of children and 5 per cent of adults have some kind of food allergy. This happens when the body's immune system incorrectly assumes a certain type of food is harmful and attacks it.

30 per cent of all the food produced in the world is never eaten, and ends up going to waste.

30 minutes at 150 degrees Celsius is the perfect amount of time and temperature you need to dry-roast peanuts.

Historic Buildings

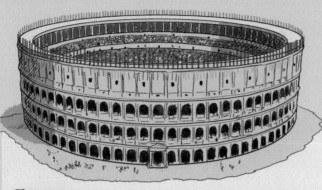

138 Egyptian pyramids have been found so far.

6 ravens live at the Tower of London, looked after by a Ravenmaster. Legend says that if the ravens desert the Tower, England itself will fall.

50,000 ancient Romans could fit in to Rome's enormous stadium called the Colosseum to watch gladiatorial contests.

2,300,000 stone blocks were used to build the Great Pyramid of Giza, in Egypt. Each one weighed between 2 and 70 tonnes.

109 years is how long it took to build a famous cathedral in Paris called Notre Dame.

6 metres of ash covered a Roman town called Pompeii when a volcano called Mount Vesuvius erupted in 79 CE. Centuries later, the town of Pompeii was rediscovered, and it is now one of the greatest Roman sites in the world.

20,000 beautiful blue tiles are the reason a mosque in Istanbul is known as The Blue Mosque.

900 bathhouses were spread throughout the city of ancient Rome by the year 300 CE.

5,000 years is the age of a burial site discovered in Denmark. There were 40 bodies inside it and 1 of them had had some early dentistry done to it.

56 kilometres away, sailors could still see light from the top of the 135-metre-high Lighthouse of Alexandria. It was built in 280 BCE in Egypt. It was so impressive that it was 1 of the 7 wonders of the ancient world (although it is now no longer standing).

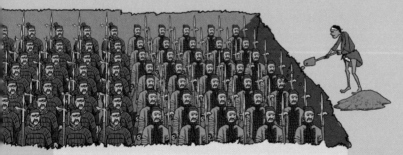

8,000 buried warriors stood guard in front of the tomb of a Chinese Emperor called Qin Shi Huang. These are known as Terracotta Warriors – life-size statues, dating from the 3rd century BCE.

118 islands, 416 bridges and 177 canals make up the historic Italian city of Venice.

201,924 kilograms is the weight of the Tsar Bell in a fortified palace in Moscow called the Kremlin. Unfortunately, it was broken while being made, so has never actually been rung.

150 ancient towns and ports have been found under the Mediterranean Sea.

400 giant stone heads gaze across the small and remote Easter Island. The heads have an average height of 4 metres and weight of 14 tonnes. The reason behind the creation of these figures is one of the world's great mysteries.

150,000 spectators could be seated in the Circus Maximus – a huge arena where the Romans held thrilling and dangerous chariot races.

63 tombs have been discovered in an area in Egypt known as Valley of the Kings, where pharaohs are buried.

8,850 kilometres is the distance covered by the Great Wall of China as it snakes its way across the Chinese countryside.

3,500 steps lead to the bottom of a well called Chand Baori in India. Built in the 10th century, it descends over 30 metres and has 13 levels.

150 shops were inside the world's first shopping centre, built in Rome by the Emperor Trajan in the 2nd century.

2,350 metres above sea level, an ancient Inca city called Machu Picchu is perched high in the mountains of Peru.

4 years were spent painting by an artist called Michelangelo, when he decorated the ceiling of the Sistine Chapel in Rome. He finally finished in 1512.

257 kilometres was the distance huge stones, some weighing up to 20 tonnes each, were transported to create a monument called Stonehenge, in England. No one knows how the ancient builders were able to carry these enormous rocks so far.

10,000 eggs were used to stick the stones together in the Bridge of Stone, found in Peru, South America. Amazingly, it is still standing after 500 years – eggs-stra-ordinary!

Asia

49 countries make up the Asian continent – from Russia in the north, to the island of Pulau Pemana in the south.

6,300 kilometres is the length of China's Yangtze River. It is the longest in Asia and the third longest in the world.

1,800 kilometres is the length of China's Grand Canal. It is the longest man-made waterway in the world.

6,540 people per square kilometre makes Hong Kong one of the most densely populated places on Earth.

15 million tourists visit a complex of palaces in Beijing called the Forbidden City each year, making it one of the least forbidden places on Earth!

136 kilograms is how much an Indonesian Komodo Dragon can weigh. They are the largest lizards on the planet.

15,000 glaciers lie in the Himalayan mountains.

390 metres below sea level is where the Dead Sea in Israel can be found. It is the lowest point on land on the planet.

3,200 tigers live in the wild. All of them are in Asia.

163 floors above ground, the tip of Dubai's Burj Khalifa skyscraper is an imposing sight. It soars 828 metres above the Arabian sands.

10 times more salt is contained in Israel's Dead Sea than in normal seawater.

70 million years is the age of the Himalayan mountain range. That might sound old, but it is actually the youngest mountain range in the world.

154,000 post offices can be found in India, giving it the most in the world.

45,000 students attend Lucknow's City Montessori School in India. The school has over 2,500 teachers and 1,000 classrooms.

1,600 giant pandas exist in the wild. They are found only in China and nowhere else on Earth.

2 Korean nations exist – North Korea and South Korea. It is not possible to travel between the two countries as this is forbidden by North Korea.

40 per cent of the population of Vietnam has the surname Nguyen.

8,848 metres is the height of Mount Everest in the Himalayas, the world's highest mountain.

2 Asian countries have populations of over 1 billion people – China and India.

660 kilometres is the length of a reservoir created by an immense dam in China called the Three Gorges Dam.

3 writing systems are used in Japanese – Hiragana, Katakana and Kanji. Hiragana is used for native Japanese words, Katakana for words taken from other languages, and Kanji are Chinese characters used to represent a word so you don't have to spell it.

1,000 films per year are produced by Bollywood – the Indian film industry based in Mumbai.

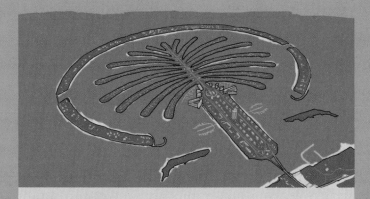

5.6 million square metres is the size of a man-made island called Palm Jumeirah in Dubai. This incredible structure is shaped like a giant palm tree.

54,000 orangutans live in Borneo and 6,000 in Sumatra.

6 times is the amount a lake in Cambodia called Tonle Sap increases in size during the rainy season.

60 active volcanoes are spread across Japan.

534 new species were discovered in the forests of Borneo between 1994 and 2007.

Amazing Art

40,000 years ago, the first artworks were created by early man on the walls of a cave in Spain, called El Castillo.

47 days was how long a famous painting by Henri Matisse was left hanging upside down in a New York art gallery before anyone noticed the mistake.

1.3 million dollars were paid at auction for a rare Chinese Ming vase. The vase had been being used as a doorstop in a house in New York.

36 million people have visited travelling exhibitions called Body Worlds, which feature real dead bodies that have been preserved and made into art.

1,000 teabags were used by a British artist called Andy Brown to make a portrait of Queen Elizabeth II.

6 million people go to view a famous painting called the Mona Lisa in Paris each year. The average time spent looking at the painting is just 15 seconds.

4 years old was the very young age of an Australian artist called Aelita Andre when she had an exhibition in New York. 3 of her paintings sold for 27,000 dollars.

1 painting was all that Vincent Van Gogh sold during his lifetime. He is now seen as one of the world's best artists, but his fame came after his death.

30 metres was the width of several giant fried eggs that were laid out across a square in Leeuwarden, Netherlands, by an artist called Henk Hofstra.

1/3 of the size of a full stop in a newspaper is the tiny size of sculptor Willard Wigan's artworks. They are so small that they fit on the head of a pin and are invisible to the naked eye.

147,800 works of art were produced by a famous Spanish artist called Pablo Picasso during his lifetime.

3.3 million Lego® bricks were used to create a life-sized, 2 storey house.

100 million individually painted porcelain sunflower seeds filled a giant hall in a gallery in London called the Tate Modern in 2010.

12 colours appear on a traditional colour wheel. These are the 3 primary colours (red, blue and yellow), the 3 secondary colours (the colours you get from mixing 2 primary colours together) and 6 tertiary colours (which are shades made by mixing a primary colour with a secondary colour).

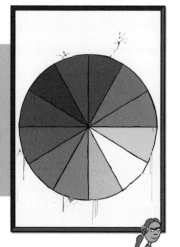

5 litres of his own, frozen blood was used by an artist called Marc Quinn to create a sculpture of his head. It first went on display in a London art gallery.

55 of the **143** paintings created by a famous Mexican artist called Frida Kahlo were self-portraits.

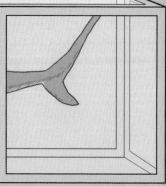

120 different colours can be found in the largest available box of Crayola® crayons. These include shades such as Jazzberry Jam, Fuzzy Wuzzy and Banana Mania.

208 metres is the height of an enormous golden statue called the Spring Temple Buddha in China. The enormous statue cost 18 million dollars to complete.

2 million works of art are housed in the permanent collection of New York's Metropolitan Museum of Art.

6,000 pounds was the amount an artist called Damien Hirst paid an Australian fisherman to catch a tiger shark for his work called The Physical Impossibility of Death in the Mind of Someone Living.

127,300 kilograms is the weight of a sculpture called The New York Earth Room, by Walter de Maria. He filled the entire second floor of a New York apartment with soil, covering 335 square metres with earth.

25 paintings make up 1 of famous artist Claude Monet's most well-known series. The images all feature haystacks. They were painted at different times of the day to see how the light and weather changed.

Pirates

3 was the number of times the tide had to come in and wash over the bodies of executed pirates who were hung on the mud flats of the River Thames in London. Only then were they declared dead and taken down.

500 dollars was the reward offered by an enraged governor to anyone who could kill a pirate called Jean Lafitte. Lafitte replied by offering triple the reward for killing the governor.

12 was the young age at which Morato Arráez joined a pirate ship and grew to become one of history's most feared pirates.

2 of the pirates on a famous pirate ship called *The Revenge* were women. They were named Anne Bonny and Mary Read.

9 knotted ropes tied to a stick made a fearsome whip for punishing pirates. It was called the cat-o'-nine-tails.

8 o'clock was bedtime for the crew members on the ship of a famous pirate known as Black Bart. His real name was Bartholomew Roberts.

900 metres was the distance a cannon could fire cannonballs into the ships of pirates' unlucky opponents.

4,000 rats were once killed by the crew on a Spanish pirate ship on a single voyage.

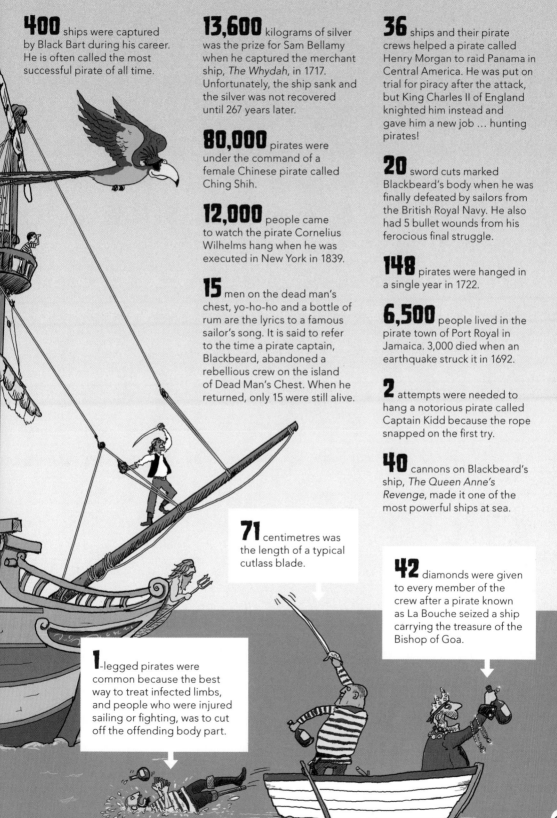

400 ships were captured by Black Bart during his career. He is often called the most successful pirate of all time.

13,600 kilograms of silver was the prize for Sam Bellamy when he captured the merchant ship, *The Whydah*, in 1717. Unfortunately, the ship sank and the silver was not recovered until 267 years later.

80,000 pirates were under the command of a female Chinese pirate called Ching Shih.

12,000 people came to watch the pirate Cornelius Wilhelms hang when he was executed in New York in 1839.

15 men on the dead man's chest, yo-ho-ho and a bottle of rum are the lyrics to a famous sailor's song. It is said to refer to the time a pirate captain, Blackbeard, abandoned a rebellious crew on the island of Dead Man's Chest. When he returned, only 15 were still alive.

36 ships and their pirate crews helped a pirate called Henry Morgan to raid Panama in Central America. He was put on trial for piracy after the attack, but King Charles II of England knighted him instead and gave him a new job … hunting pirates!

20 sword cuts marked Blackbeard's body when he was finally defeated by sailors from the British Royal Navy. He also had 5 bullet wounds from his ferocious final struggle.

148 pirates were hanged in a single year in 1722.

6,500 people lived in the pirate town of Port Royal in Jamaica. 3,000 died when an earthquake struck it in 1692.

2 attempts were needed to hang a notorious pirate called Captain Kidd because the rope snapped on the first try.

40 cannons on Blackbeard's ship, *The Queen Anne's Revenge*, made it one of the most powerful ships at sea.

71 centimetres was the length of a typical cutlass blade.

42 diamonds were given to every member of the crew after a pirate known as La Bouche seized a ship carrying the treasure of the Bishop of Goa.

1-legged pirates were common because the best way to treat infected limbs, and people who were injured sailing or fighting, was to cut off the offending body part.

Cool Caves

20 million bats live in the Bracken Bat Cave in Texas, USA. Every night they swarm out in a cloud so huge it takes 3 hours for all the bats to emerge from the cave.

85-100 tonnes of bat guano (poo) is deposited at the Bracken Bat Cave each year. This is harvested and sold as fertilizer for crops and plants.

1 metre is the wingspan of a Bulmer's fruit bat, the world's largest cave-dwelling bat. It was thought to be extinct until some were discovered in a remote cave in Papua New Guinea.

44 degrees Celsius is the sweltering temperature inside the Cave of Crystals in Mexico. This cave is the hottest in the world.

50,000 different species of troglobite are thought to exist. A troglobite is an animal that lives its whole life in a cave and does not venture out.

150 metres was the length of a journey Carlos Coste made through a Mexican cave. The cave was underwater, and Carlos swam through it without any breathing apparatus.

560 kilometres of the Mammoth Cave system in Kentucky, USA, have so far been explored. An estimated 966 kilometres remain to be surveyed.

8,000 images of Buddha can be found in the amazing Pindaya Caves in Burma.

186 pupils attended the Dongzhong school in China. It was named because it was housed in the Dongzhong Cave until 2011.

24,000 soldiers were housed in caves beneath a French city called Arras during World War I. The army built a hospital, canteens and even a railway inside the cave.

427 metres is the distance you would fall straight down if you fell into the mouth of the Cave of the Swallows in Mexico.

8 jumbo jet planes could easily fit inside the Sarawak Chamber in Malaysia. The cave chamber is 700 metres long, 400 metres wide and 100 metres high.

2,196 metres below sea level was the depth a caving team reached when exploring the world's deepest cave at Krubera in Georgia, USA.

6,646 metres above sea level is the height of a cave found by climbers on the Rakhiot Peak in Pakistan. It is the highest cave in the world.

8.2 metres is the length of a stalactite on the roof in the Jeita Grotto in Lebanon. A stalactite is an icicle-shaped mineral structure that hangs down from the ceiling of a cave.

60 metres is the height of a huge stalagmite (a mineral feature that grows up from the ground of a cave) in a cave in Cuba called the Martin Inferno Cave. That's about the same height as the Leaning Tower of Pisa in Italy.

69 different animals were identified among the fossils found by an Australian scientist when he slipped into a pot hole and discovered an unknown cave. The fossils included birds, reptiles, lions and kangaroos.

73 metres is the height of an underground waterfall in La Grotte aux Fées (The Cave of the Fairies) in Switzerland.

2,000 figures appear in some incredible cave art found in the Lascaux caves in France. The 20,000-year-old paintings include 364 horses and 90 stags.

8.2 kilometres is the distance the Puerto Princesa River, in the Philippines, runs underground through caves until it reaches the sea.

603 metres is the height of a sheer drop inside the Vrtoglavica Cave in Slovenia. This is nearly twice the height of the Eiffel Tower, in Paris.

272 steps lead up to the entrance to the Batu caves in Malaysia. Visitors are often accompanied by monkeys in their climb to the top.

30 cave towns are spread across a region of Turkey called Cappadocia. The rock was so soft that thousands of years ago, people dug their homes in the ground. Some of the cave houses are still occupied, and there are even some cave hotels.

35 days was how long a Frenchman called Jean-Luc Josuat spent lost in a cave after taking a wrong turn. He lived in complete darkness and ate wood and clay until he was finally rescued by 3 teenagers who were exploring the cave.

319 metres below the surface lies the bed of a lake in a cavity in the ground called a sinkhole, at El Zacatón in Mexico. It was only in 2007 that geologists discovered the bed of this famous bottomless lake.

67 metres below ground is where you'll find the Grand Cavern cave motel room. It has beds, a sofa, tables, chairs, a bathroom and everything else you would expect from a hotel.

Natural Disasters

1,170 degrees Celsius is the temperature reached by lava when it flows out of a volcano – that's hot enough to melt most metals.

65,000 cubic metres of water (around 26 Olympic-sized swimming pools' worth) moved every single second during a 1927 Mississippi river flood.

12,700 kilometres was the distance covered by Hurricane Faith in 1966. The hurricane began off the coast of Africa and swept across the Atlantic Ocean.

5 different categories of hurricane are listed on a scale called the Saffir-Simpson scale, which measures hurricanes by wind speed. Category 5, the nastiest, features speeds of over 250 kilometres per hour.

130,000 square kilometres were flooded when the Huang He river in China burst its banks in 1887. That's an area almost as large as Greece.

800 kilometres per hour is the speed at which a tsunami wave can move across the open ocean.

1,550 metres was the amount by which Mount Tambora, in Indonesia shrank when it erupted in 1815. It stood at around 4,300 metres tall before the eruption, but afterwards it was just 2,851 metres in height.

398 metres is the distance that 19-year-old Matt Suter was carried by a tornado in 2006. He survived to tell the tale.

2 million hectares were burned during a devastating wildfire in Victoria, Australia in 1939. That's about half the area of Denmark. The fires became known as the Black Friday fires.

75 billion dollars of damage was believed to have been caused by a devastating hurricane called Katrina in 2005.

5 letters are not used by the World Meteorological Organization when naming hurricanes because of the limited number of names they offer. These are Q, U, X, Y and Z.

14 different countries were affected by a deadly tsunami that began after an earthquake in the Indian Ocean on December 26th, 2004. More than 200,000 people lost their lives in the disaster.

250 million dump trucks would have been needed to cart away all the rocks that fell in a landslide caused by an eruption of the Mount St Helens volcano in Washington, USA.

130 kilometres per hour is the speed that a large mass of snow and ice can reach within just 5 seconds of an avalanche starting.

90 per cent of all the world's earthquakes occur in an area surrounding the edges of the Pacific Ocean, known as the Ring of Fire.

830,000 people are believed to have died in Shansi, China, in 1556, when a powerful earthquake struck the region. It is thought to have been the most devastating earthquake ever.

32 kilometres was the height that ash that was sent up into the atmosphere when Novarupta, a volcano in Alaska, USA, erupted in 1912. This is more than twice the height at which aeroplanes fly.

4,800 kilometres away was the distance from which people could hear the eruption of a volcano called Krakatoa in Indonesia, in 1883. It's said to be the loudest sound in history.

148 tornadoes occurred in 13 US states on April 3rd and 4th, 1974. Known as a super outbreak, these tornadoes caused the loss of 330 lives.

2 people in the town of St Pierre on the Caribbean island of Martinique survived the 1902 eruption of Mt Pelée. 1 was a prisoner locked in a prison cell with thick stone walls. More than 20,000 people perished.

93 per cent of people buried in avalanches should survive if they are dug out within 15 minutes.

4 out of **4** engines on a British Airways Boeing 747 airliner heading for Australia in 1982 stopped working when volcanic ash clogged its engines. The pilot, Captain Eric Moody, remained calm and let the plane glide on no power for 15 minutes before the engines could be restarted.

20 per cent of the 500,000 earthquakes that occur every year can be felt by humans. Only 100 or so a year cause any damage.

1,500 kilometres was the diameter of the enormous Hurricane Sandy in 2012.

50 metres is the height that the Paracutin volcanic cone grew out of a Mexican cornfield in just 24 hours in 1943. It doubled in height in a week as it continued to erupt, and when it finished 9 years later it was 424 metres tall.

0-5 is the range of the Fujita measurement scale of tornadoes. It rates them by the amount of destruction they cause. An F5 tornado can rip buildings from their foundations and fling cars and trucks through the air.

2 million football pitches is the approximate area of land cleared by wildfires in the United States every year.

1,717 tornadoes occurred in the United States in 2004, a record year.

Super Sports

2.7 million bananas were eaten by the athletes at the 2012 Olympic and Paralympic games in London.

6 grams of gold are found in a modern Olympic gold medal. The rest of the medal is made mostly of silver with a little copper.

10 centimetres is the width of a balance beam in gymnastics. Gymnasts perform giant leaps and somersaults but must land safely on the very narrow beam.

183 individual games were played in a tennis match at Wimbledon in 2010, between John Isner and Nicolas Mahut. Isner finally won the match, which lasted over 11 hours.

49 kilograms is the minimum weight of a woman that is carried by a man around an obstacle course in the World Wife Carrying Championships.

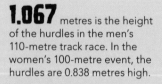

1.067 metres is the height of the hurdles in the men's 110-metre track race. In the women's 100-metre event, the hurdles are 0.838 metres high.

2 seconds is all it took for 21-year-old Saudi Arabian footballer Nawaf Al Abed to score a goal straight from the kick-off in 2009.

7.260 kilograms is the weight of a shot, the heavy metal ball that athletes throw in the shot put event. That's about as heavy as 2 bricks.

22 balls are placed on a snooker table at the start of a frame – 15 red balls, 6 coloured balls and 1 white ball, known as the cue ball.

105.4 laps of a 400-metre running track would be necessary to complete a marathon race.

10 minutes after becoming the manager of Torquay United football club in 2007, Leroy Rosenoir was sacked. Someone had bought the football club and brought in a new manager.

31 goals were scored by Australia as they thrashed American Samoa in a FIFA World Cup qualifying match in 2001. Australia's Archie Thompson scored 13 of these goals.

149 own goals were scored by 1 team, Stade Olympique L'Emyrne in a football match, against fellow Madagascan team, A.S. Adema in 2002.

2.7 grams is the weight of a table tennis ball. Top players can smash the ball at speeds of over 80 kilometres per hour.

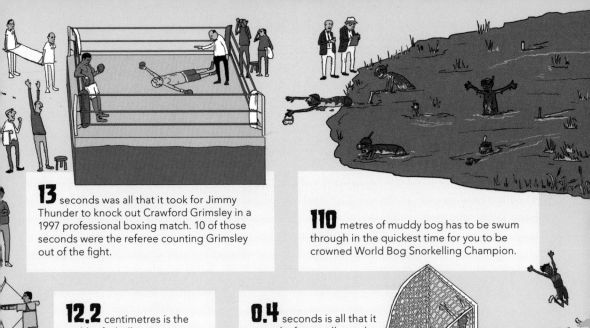

13 seconds was all that it took for Jimmy Thunder to knock out Crawford Grimsley in a 1997 professional boxing match. 10 of those seconds were the referee counting Grimsley out of the fight.

110 metres of muddy bog has to be swum through in the quickest time for you to be crowned World Bog Snorkelling Champion.

12.2 centimetres is the width of a bullseye on an Olympic archery target. Archers have to try to hit the target from 70 metres away.

0.4 seconds is all that it can take for a well-struck penalty kick to reach the back of the net in a football match.

320 kilometres per hour is the speed a shuttlecock can reach when hit by a top badminton player. That's faster than a high-speed train.

5,420 seconds was all that it took for David Weir to win the 2012 Paralympics men's marathon. Weir averaged a speed of over 28 kilometres per hour.

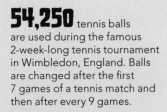

54,250 tennis balls are used during the famous 2-week-long tennis tournament in Wimbledon, England. Balls are changed after the first 7 games of a tennis match and then after every 9 games.

700 minutes was the length of 1 wrestling bout at the 1912 Olympics. The winner, Martin Klein, got through to the final but was too exhausted to compete, so he had to settle for a silver medal.

3.75 million litres of water (around 46,875 bath-tubs' worth) is the minimum required to fill up an Olympic-sized swimming pool which is 50 metres long.

6.1 metres was the winning distance managed by Constant van Langendonck and his horse, Extra-Dry, in the 1900 Olympic Horse Long Jump competition – the first and only time the event was part of the Olympics.

6 players take part in each team in an Octopush game on the bottom of a 25-metre-long swimming pool. The players use sticks to push a puck along the floor of the pool, trying to score goals at either end.

15 kilograms of pork sausages was the unusual transfer fee paid by a Romanian football club called Regal Hornia to buy a footballer named Marius Cioara in 2006.

Space Travel

120 seconds after lift-off, a Space Shuttle would already be approximately 45 kilometres above the Earth.

135 missions into space were flown by NASA's fleet of Space Shuttle spacecraft between 1981 and 2011.

569 kilometres is the height that the Hubble Space Telescope orbits above the Earth's surface. It was launched in 1990.

826.72 million

kilometres is the total distance in space travelled by NASA's fleet of Space Shuttle. This is the distance from the Earth to Jupiter.

536 minutes is the amount of time that astronauts Susan Helms and Jim Voss spent outside their spacecraft on a spacewalk in 2001.

13,000 people applied to become the first British astronaut. The winner was Helen Sharman, a 27-year-old British chemist, who went into space in 1991 in a Russian Soyuz spacecraft after 18 months of training.

400,171 kilometres is the furthest distance that humans have ever travelled from the Earth. It was reached by the crew of a spacecraft called *Apollo 13* in 1970.

3,941 kilograms of fuel was used by a *Saturn V* space rocket every second during lift-off.

424 kilobytes was all the computer memory that the Space Shuttles' computers had. That's thousands of times less than the memory found in a modern mobile phone.

18.4 billion kilometres is the distance that a space probe called *Voyager 1* is from the Earth. It was launched in 1977 and, by the end of 2012, it was 123 times further away from the Earth than the average distance between the Earth and the Sun.

162 spacewalks (trips that astronauts take outside their spacecraft) have been made to build and service the International Space Station (ISS).

65,000 parts make up the *Voyager 1* space probe. It launched in 1977 and nearly all of the parts are still working!

3,630 kilograms of food has to be carried into space to feed a crew of 3 people on a 6-month-long visit to the International Space Station (known as the ISS).

14 million

pounds was the price paid by Dennis Tito to become the first space tourist. Tito spent 8 days on board the International Space Station, in 2001, as part of a Russian mission.

108 minutes were spent in space by the first astronaut, Yuri Gagarin, in 1961. His spacecraft was called *Vostok 1*.

18 metres taller than the Statue of Liberty, was the height of an enormous *Saturn V* rocket. These rockets were used to launch *Apollo* missions to the Moon.

36 years after his first spaceflight in 1962, John Glenn, aged 77, became the oldest astronaut when he took part in a Space Shuttle mission in 1998.

3.5 billion kilometres was the distance through space that the *Cassini* space probe travelled to reach Saturn. That's more than 20 times the distance from the Earth to the Sun.

23 different dishes were served in a gourmet feast on board the *Mir* space station in 1988 including pigeon stew and duck with artichokes.

6 o'clock is the time that the astronauts in the International Space Station are woken up by an alarm clock signal beamed from the Earth. It's an early start for spacemen and women!

91.5 metres of tubes carry cooling water around the underwear worn by an astronaut on a spacewalk.

120 gigabytes of scientific data is sent from the Hubble Space Telescope back to the Earth every week – enough to fill books requiring over 1,000 metres of shelf space.

19,000 pieces of space junk orbit the Earth, including an astronaut's lost glove, nuts and bolts and fragments of destroyed satellites.

12 metres was the height that the first liquid-fueled rocket reached after its launch in 1926.

35,000 kilometres per hour was the top speed reached by the first *Ariane V* rocket, launched in 1999. That's about 100 times faster than the fastest sports car.

803 days is the most time spent in space by an astronaut. Sergei Krikalev enjoyed 2 missions to the *Mir* space station, 2 Space Shuttle missions and 1 trip to the International Space Station.

400 adult African elephants would weigh the same as a loaded *Saturn V* rocket – that's a total of around 2.8 million kilograms.

Fun Festivals

12 days is the length of time Christians celebrate Christmas. December 25th is the first day of Christmas and January 6th is the twelfth day.

100 million people attend the Hindu festival of Kumbh Mela. It takes place for 55 days once every 12 years on the banks of India's River Ganges at Allahabad.

1 month of fasting happens between sunrise and sunset during a Muslim festival called Ramadan. It is followed by Id al-Fitr, the feast of fast-breaking.

200,000 people take part in New York's annual St Patrick's Day Parade.

300 music bands take part in a famous Carnival parade in Rio, Brazil.

7,000 cockroach fans attend the annual day of cockroach racing in Brisbane, Australia.

63.1 metres was the length of a huge Christmas cracker pulled by the children of an English school in 2001.

50,000 camels are brought to an annual camel fair in India. The camels are beautifully decorated by their owners for the event.

500,000 king cakes are sold during a festival called Mardi Gras in New Orleans, USA, each year. Every cake contains a tiny doll, and the person who finds it is declared the king. They have to buy the next cake or give a party.

8 days is the length of a Jewish festival called Hannukah. A candelabrum holds 9 candles and the candle in the centre, called a shammus, is used to light the others. Each day, a new candle is lit in a candle holder, until all 9 are alight.

1 out of the millions of turkeys eaten at the American feast of Thanksgiving is very lucky. Each year, the National Turkey Federation presents a live turkey to the President, who pardons it. The bird then spends the rest of its life in comfort on a farm.

1,000 torch bearers march through town during a Viking festival called Up Helly Aa in Scotland's Shetland Islands. At the end of the march, the torches are thrown into a Viking longship and crowds gather to watch the ship burn.

8,000 rioters stormed a Paris prison called the Bastille on July 14th, 1789, at the beginning of the French Revolution. July 14th is now known as Bastille Day and is a public holiday and day of celebration in France.

1 million kites soar into the sky during the Ahmedabad Kite Festival in India.

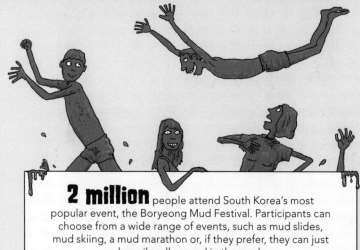

12 animals are included in the cycle of Chinese years. Each Chinese New Year has 1 of the following signs: rat, ox, tiger, rabbit, dragon, snake, horse, goat, monkey, rooster, dog and pig.

4 days is the length of Songkran, Thailand's New Year celebration. As it is traditional to drench people with water, it is also one of the world's largest water fights.

2 million people attend South Korea's most popular event, the Boryeong Mud Festival. Participants can choose from a wide range of events, such as mud slides, mud skiing, a mud marathon or, if they prefer, they can just happily roll around in the mud.

1 million people visit the 10-day Calgary Stampede, the world's biggest rodeo show, held in Canada each year.

120 metres long and 48 metres high is the size some ice sculptures can reach at Harbin Ice Festival in China. Over 13 million people travel to see these chilly works of art.

29,381 pumpkins, also known as jack-o'-lanterns, were lit during the 2012 Keene Pumpkin Festival in New Hampshire, USA. The carved pumpkins were presented in a spectacular, glowing tower.

77,282 fireworks exploded in the sky as part of the celebrations for Kuwait's 50th anniversary in 2012.

700 hot air balloons take off and fill the sky at the world's largest hot air balloon festival in Albuquerque, USA.

30,000 cherry blossom trees cover Yoshino-yama Mountain. It is one of the best places to witness the Japanese Cherry Blossom Festival. When these beautiful trees bloom, Japanese families celebrate by holding parties underneath them.

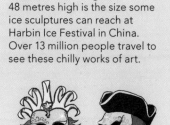

2 men – Napoleon and Mussolini – have tried to ban the Venice Carnival, but it still continues. Every February, the city is full of beautifully dressed people wearing masks.

5 days after the beginning of the fifth month in the Chinese lunar calendar is the date for the Chinese Dragon Boat Festival. Celebrations include the racing of dragon boats which may be up to 30 metres long and have 80 paddlers.

20,000 people gather at an ancient ruin called Stonehenge in England at the summer solstice (the longest day of the year) to watch the sun rise.

2,000 monkeys attend Thailand's Monkey Buffet Festival. Local people prepare a feast of food for the monkeys living at the Pra Prang Sam Yot temple.

Numbers

8 is regarded as the luckiest number in China. Some people even pay extra to have a telephone number containing the number 8.

0 as a number didn't exist for a long time. It only came about as the figure 0 we know today in India in around the year 900.

0.01 seconds is a unit of time actually known as a jiffy.

7 is the number that opposites sides of a dice always add up to.

13 is considered unlucky by so many people in the Western world, there is even a name given to the fear of it – triskaidekaphobia.

666 is bad luck in Western culture, as it is associated with Satan in the Christian Bible. However, in Asia, the pronunciation of 666 sounds very much like the phrase: things going smoothly. This means it is considered to be lucky.

12,345,678,987,654,321 is the answer to the sum 111,111,111 x 111,111,111. The sequence of numbers is 1 to 9 and back to 1.

4 is an unlucky number in the Far East. The pronunciation of the number in Japanese is very similar to the word death, and is considered bad luck in Japan, Korea and China.

1 followed by a googol zeros is called a googolplex. This is a number so enormous that it is impossible to write down – there is not enough space in the whole Universe to fit it in.

∞ is the symbol for infinity. Infinity refers to something without limit, a never-ending number.

NOOOO! I THINK I'VE LOST COUNT.

31,688 years is the length of time it would take you to count to 1 trillion if you counted continuously for every moment of every day.